However,

However,
The Painful Process of Pruning.

Rhondnita Reed

No Sugar Coat Press

For Grandma Georgia and Aunt Shirley.

You were my safe place, my strong place, and my foundation.

Everything I became started with what you poured into me.

I am living well to honor you both.

Forever your Rhondnita.

It is an imperfect book written by an imperfect person downloaded by a perfect God trying to reach the next imperfect person.

— Rhondnita Reed

Who Holds the Pen?

That is a fair question.

And you deserve an honest answer before you go any further.

The woman holding this pen is not a theologian. She is not a celebrity pastor or a bestselling author or someone who found these words in a quiet moment of inspiration with a cup of tea and a view of the mountains.

She is a 53-year-old educator who has been through some things.

Some real things.

She has been a single mother — learning what it means to be everything for someone else when you are not sure you have enough left for yourself. She has loved people who hurt her — not once but twice — in ways that took years to understand and longer to heal. She has survived a divorce. She has been betrayed by family. The kind of betrayal that doesn't just end a relationship — it ends something in you that takes a long time to name. She has navigated marriage. She has raised children who tested every boundary she had. She has sat with a sick child in the middle of the night and still shown up for other people's children in the morning. She earned four degrees while surviving. The last one completed in eighteen months — through 2022, through major surgery the day before her final semester began, through everything that year tried to take from her. She refused to stay an extra semester. She refused to accept anything less than an A. She earned it. She launched not one but two businesses — the first one in 2020, when the whole world was shutting down, and everything said this is the wrong time.

She has felt like a failure.

She has compared herself to others and come up short in her own eyes.

She has looked at what she had and decided it wasn't enough.

And she has kept going anyway.

Not because she had it figured out. Not because the road got easier. But because somewhere in the middle of the hard — in the middle of the pruning — words started surfacing. Not planned words. Not rehearsed words. Words that came up from the inside because she was living them in real time.

Those words became sayings.

Those sayings became this book.

So who holds this pen?

A woman who has been pruned. Shaped. Tested. Carried. And is still here — not in spite of the hard, but because of what the hard produced in her.

A woman who stopped doing it alone and learned to do it along — with a God who has been faithful through every single season this list represents.

A woman who is me. Fully. Flaws and all.

And if any part of that list sounded familiar — if you saw yourself somewhere in those lines — then I want you to know something.

I didn't write this book for the woman who has it all together.

I wrote it for the woman who is still in it. Still standing. Still breathing. Still wondering if the hard is ever going to produce anything worth all of this.

It will.

I am living proof.

Now turn the page. We have work to do.

— Rhondnita

Author's Note

I learned a long time ago not to sugarcoat or hide who Rhondnita truly is. I am me, and I am okay with her. Flaws and all.

This book was not born in a writing class or a publisher's office. It was not born from a platform or an opportunity or anyone's permission. It was born in a conversation — the kind where you are working through something out loud and God downloads something into your spirit so clearly that you cannot pretend you did not hear it.

Write it down. Somewhere permanent. Plain. No sugarcoating.

And so I did.

I want to be clear about what you are holding. This is not a perfect book. It was written by an imperfect person, downloaded by a perfect God, trying to reach the next imperfect person. It is not a theology degree. It is not a self-help manual. It is not a highlight reel of someone who figured it all out and came back to tell you how.

It is a testimony. A lived one.

I don't know about bulletproof faith — I do know about lived faith.

The kind of faith that does not look good on a highlight reel but shows up anyway. The kind that gets tested in real time, in real seasons, with real loss and real hard and real moments where the only prayer you have left is I'm here. That is the faith this book was written from. And that is the faith it was written for.

This journey did not happen overnight. It is the culmination of years and decades of living with hard, difficult, and different. Of pruning seasons that felt like punishment before they revealed themselves as preparation. Of a God who never once promised easy but always provided enough.

This book is not about me. It is despite of me.

I did not tell anyone I was writing this book. This book was written in quiet, in honesty, in the spaces between everything else that needed my attention. It was written for the person who needed to know that hard is not the end. That different is not a shortcoming. That the pruning is not punishment. That you can survive the hard season and come out on the other side still standing, still faithful, still you.

However, is not just the title. It is the theology. It is the comma that sits between the hard and the keep going. It is the word that refuses to let the difficult have the last say.

However, Keep going.

I am Rhondnita. This is my however, and I wrote it down so you would know yours is possible too.

Preface

This book is going to ask something of you.

It is going to ask you to be honest. Not the polished kind of honest that sounds good in a conversation, but the raw kind that sits with you at two in the morning when nobody else is around. It is going to ask you to look at the hard things in your life not as stop signs but as commas. It is going to ask you to keep going when every part of you wants to stop.

It is not going to be comfortable. It was not written to be comfortable. It was written to be true.

But before you turn to Chapter 1, I need you to hear something first.

You are worth the journey you are about to go on.

Not when you get it together. Not when the hard season is over. Not when you have enough faith or enough strength or enough distance from whatever brought you to this book in the first place. Right now. Exactly as you are. Flaws and all. Hard and all. However, and all.

You are worth it.

This book will not do the work for you. It will walk alongside you while you do it. It will tell you the truth when the truth is hard to hear. It will remind you that the pruning is not punishment and the different is not wrong and the hard is not the end.

And when you get to the last page — and you will get to the last page — you will know something you did not know when you opened this one.

That you were always worth the journey.

However, Keep going

HOWEVER,

The Painful Process of Pruning

Introduction

A breath before we begin

Congratulations.

I mean that sincerely.

The fact that you are holding this book — that you opened the cover and made it to this page — that is not a small thing. For some of you, this was the easy part. You saw the title, felt something stir, and dove in without hesitation.

But for some of you — and I know you are out there — just getting here took everything you had. Maybe someone gave you this book, and it sat on your nightstand for three weeks before you picked it up. Maybe you downloaded it and let it live on your device unopened because something in you knew that opening it meant starting something you weren't sure you were ready for.

You opened it anyway.

That is the however comma in action before you even read the first chapter. The pause between the hard thing and the forward motion. The breath that says — *this is difficult and I am doing it anyway.*

So yes. Congratulations. You showed up. That matters.

Now I need to tell you something before we go any further.

However, is not about tutus and rainbows.

I need you to hear that clearly before you turn another page. There are plenty of books that will hold your hand and tell you everything is going to be okay and send you on your way feeling warm and fuzzy and largely unchanged. *However,* is not one of them.

This book is going to dig deep.

It is going to hurt in places you forgot were tender. It is going to make you angry — at yourself, at your circumstances, at the excuses you have been carrying so long they started to feel like facts. It is going to ask something of you that you may not even know you possess yet.

And it is going to be worth every uncomfortable page.

Because on the other side of the discomfort is the bloom. The thing the pruning was always working toward. The life that has been waiting on the other side of the hard you have been avoiding.

Here is how *However,* works.

There are fourteen sayings. Each one was born from a real moment in a real life — my life — and each one has been tested in the fire before it made it to this page. They are not motivational posters. They are not things that sound good from a comfortable distance. They are survival notes. Written in the middle of the hard and handed to you now because you are in the middle of yours.

The book is divided into four parts. Each part has an introduction — a breath before the next section begins. Not to soften what is coming. But to prepare you for it. There is a difference.

At the end of each chapter, you will find a closing prayer and five discussion questions. Use them. Don't skip them. They are where the real work happens. In the quiet after the reading. In the journal. In the small group. In the honest conversation with yourself at 2 am when nobody else is listening.

One more thing.

If you make it through Part One — the rest gets easier. I promise you that.

Part One is the hardest section of *However,* it is confrontational in the most loving way I know how to be. It will remove your excuses one by one until you are standing in the open with nothing left to hide behind. It will look you in the eye and tell you the truth about hard and yet and fear and what it actually means to begin.

It will ask more of you than you think you have.

And it will find out — the same way life has always found out — that you have more than you think.

So take a breath.

Plant your feet.

Turn the page.

However, **— here we go.**

Part One

The Courage to Begin

A breath before Part One

Can I be honest with you about something?

Beginning is the hardest part.

Not the middle. Not the end. The beginning. The moment before the first step, when everything in you is screaming every reason why now is not the right time, you are not the right person, and this is not the right season.

That voice is not wisdom. That voice is fear dressed up in reasonable clothing. And Part One of *However,* is about taking off the costume and seeing it for what it actually is.

These four chapters are going to challenge everything you believe about hard and yet and fear and what it means to do something anyway. They are going to ask you to look at the excuses you have been using to stay comfortable and call them what they are. They are going to invite you — firmly and lovingly and without apology — to take the first step.

Not the whole journey. Just the first step.

Here is what Part One is not going to do.

It is not going to pretend the beginning is easy. It is not going to tell you that if you just believe hard enough the hard will disappear. It is not going to hand you a five-step formula for instant courage.

Real courage doesn't work that way.

Real courage is the woman who opens the book anyway. Real courage is the student who picks up the pencil anyway. Real courage is the person who takes the first step anyway — not because the fear is gone, but because the destination matters more than the fear.

Real courage is the however comma lived out loud.

Part One has four chapters. Four sayings. Four different angles on the same essential truth —

Hard is not a reason to stop. Yet is not a sign of weakness. Fear is not as big as it feels. And you cannot ask others to do what you are not willing to do yourself.

By the time you finish Part One, you will have run out of reasons not to begin.

And that is exactly the point.

Take a breath.

Part One of *However*, starts now.

HOWEVER,

The Painful Process of Pruning

Chapter 1

"Hard doesn't mean don't do it — Hard means do it anyway."

Before we begin

I need you to know something before we go any further.

I am not writing this from a quiet place of having it all together. I am not a woman who found these words in a season of stillness and decided to share them with the world. I found these words the same way most real things are found — in the middle of a mess, on the floor, wondering how I was going to get back up.

I have been a single mother. I have loved people who hurt me — not once but twice — in ways that took years to understand and longer to heal. I have been betrayed by family. The kind of betrayal that doesn't just break a relationship — it breaks something in you that took a long time to name. I have survived a divorce. I have navigated marriage troubles that required more honesty than I sometimes felt capable of. I launched a business during a global pandemic when the whole world was shutting down, and nothing made sense. I have felt like a failure. I have compared myself to others and come up short in my own eyes. I have looked at what I had and decided it wasn't enough — and then treated it like it wasn't.

And through every single one of those seasons — I kept going.

Not because I was strong. Not because I had a plan. Not because I wasn't scared or tired or convinced some days that I simply could not take another step. I kept going because somewhere deep in me — deeper than the fear, deeper than the exhaustion, deeper than the wounds — something kept saying *not yet. Keep moving. Do it anyway.*

I didn't know what to call that something for a long time.

Now I do.

These sayings are not things I came up with at a desk. They are things that surfaced in the middle of real moments — real pain, real confusion, real grief, real joy. They came up the way truth tends to come up — uninvited, unpolished, and exactly on time.

So if you picked up this book because something in the title felt like it was written for you — I want you to know.

It was.

I am me, and I am okay with her. Flaws and all. And by the time you finish this book — my prayer is that you can say the same thing about yourself.

The moment it was born

It was a Monday night in March. Nothing dramatic on the outside. Just a notification. A cancellation. My therapist. No explanation. The night before my scheduled session.

That's all it was on paper.

But I know what it was. It wasn't just an inconvenience. It landed on an old wound — the one that knows the specific weight of people leaving without warning. Without reason. Without care for what they leave behind. I had been brave enough to pursue counseling. Vulnerable enough to show up. And now this.

I sat with it. I processed the disappointment, the familiar sting of feeling let down, the quiet voice that whispered *maybe this isn't worth it. Maybe nothing is.*

And then — almost casually. Like it was the most obvious thing in the world — I said it.

Hard doesn't mean don't do it — Hard means do it anyway.

I didn't plan it. I didn't rehearse it. I didn't find it in someone else's book or see it on a motivational poster. It came up from inside me because I was living it in that exact moment. That's the only place real wisdom ever comes from.

I even surprised myself. *I just came up with that.*

Yes. I did. Because sometimes the truest things we know don't arrive through study — they arrive through survival.

But here is what I need you to understand.

That saying didn't start on that Monday night in March.

It started in 2006.

The Pruning

In 2006, I went through my first divorce. And if you have been through one, you already know — divorce is the pruning that doesn't ask your permission. It doesn't come with a warning label or a timeline or a guarantee of what grows back. It just comes. And it cuts. And it hurts in places you didn't even know were alive until they were bleeding.

I want to talk to you about pruning for a moment. Because I believe it is the most honest way to describe what hard actually is.

If you have ever watched someone prune a rose bush, you know it looks violent. It looks wrong. You are cutting back something living. Something that was growing. And when it is done, the bush looks bare and exposed and honestly — worse than before.

But the gardener knows something the bush doesn't.

The cutting is not the ending. The cutting is the beginning.

Without the pruning, the bush stays alive, but it never reaches its full bloom. It survives. It functions. But it never becomes what it was created to be. The pruning — the painful uncomfortable necessary pruning — is what produces the flowers.

Hard is the pruning.

And here is the thing about God that nobody puts in the brochure —

He will show you the problem. He has already prepared the provision. But what He doesn't always tell you about is the middle part. The part between the problem and the provision. The part that requires everything you have and then asks for a little more.

That middle part is the process. That process is the pruning. And the pruning — as painful as it is — is not punishment.

It is preparation.

Alone versus along

After my divorce in 2006, I spent fourteen years in that middle part. And I want to be honest with you about what those fourteen years looked like — because I think you need to hear this.

I was not idle. I was not sitting still waiting for God to show up. I earned three degrees. I raised two children — a daughter who tested every boundary I had and a son with severe allergies and asthma who kept me in a constant state of alert. I learned to love again, and in 2009, I married a man who has been there. I survived. I showed up. Every single day.

By every visible measure, I was moving forward.

But here is the distinction I need you to sit with.

There is a difference between doing it **alone** and doing it **along.**

Alone — just one letter away from along — is you operating in your own strength. Your degrees. Your hustle. Your survival skills. Your ability to figure it out. And alone can produce impressive things. Three degrees are impressive. Raising children through hard seasons is impressive. Getting up every day when you have every reason not to — that is impressive.

But along is different.

Along means doing it with God. Fully surrendered to what He specifically called you to. Not just surviving — but stepping into the thing He designed you for before you were born. Along means trusting the pruning even when it hurts. It means moving forward into the uncomfortable because God is in it — not because it feels safe.

The hard of staying put — and I want to be clear about what staying put really means — is not that you stop accomplishing things. You can be fully busy and still be staying put. You can have degrees and a career and a full calendar and still be staying put. Because staying put means choosing your own comfortable accomplishments over the uncomfortable thing God called you to specifically.

Activity is not the same as alignment.

And for fourteen years, I was active. Impressively active. But I was hesitant to do it along with God. Hesitant to step fully into the uncomfortable. Hesitant to trust the pruning with my whole self.

Then 2020 came.

A global pandemic. The whole world was shutting down. Everything uncertain. Everything frightening. Everything saying *this is the wrong time.*

And that is exactly when I launched my first business.

Not because it made sense. Not because the circumstances were favorable. But because the fourteen years of underground growth had finally produced enough root that the bloom could no longer be contained.

2024 brought the second business.

And on a Monday night in March — in the middle of a hard moment that had nothing to do with business — the words finally came.

Hard doesn't mean don't do it. Hard means do it anyway.

What hard is not

Before we go further, I need to clear something up.

Hard is not a sign that you are going the wrong direction. Hard is not God's way of closing a door. Hard is not weakness. Hard is not punishment.

Hard is not the obstacle between you and the life God has for you.

Hard is the process of getting there.

And here is the choice that sits in front of every one of us in every hard season —

You can choose the hard of moving forward. Or you can choose the hard of staying put.

Because here is what nobody tells you — staying put has its own hard. Its own cost. Its own consequences. The woman who never gets pruned stays alive but never fully blooms. She accomplishes things but delays the specific things God designed her for. She survives, but she does not step into the supernatural.

There is no option that costs you nothing.

There is only the question of which hard you choose.

The hard that leads somewhere. Or the hard of staying exactly where you are.

This is the beginning not the end

I need you to hear this clearly before you turn the page.

Hard is not the ending of your story.

Hard is the beginning of the next chapter of it.

Every hard season in my life — the divorce, the single motherhood, the four degrees earned in survival mode, the abusive relationships, the betrayal, the business launched in a pandemic — every single one of them felt like an ending while I was in it. It felt like the pruning would never stop. Like the bare exposed bush was all I would ever be.

But the gardener knew.

And God knows.

The cutting is not the conclusion. The cutting is the preparation. The hard is not the period at the end of your sentence.

The hard is the comma.

However,

Keep going.

A Prayer for the Hard

Lord, you never promised easy. You promised present. You promised through. On the days when the pruning is painful, and I cannot see what You are growing — remind me that You are the gardener and You know exactly what You are doing. Give me the faith to trust the process. Give me the courage to choose the hard of moving forward over the hard of staying put. Let my doing it anyway be an act of surrender, not just survival.

And when the bloom finally comes — let me remember the cutting that made it possible. Amen.

Questions for reflection

1. Where in your life right now are you choosing the hard of staying put over the hard of moving forward? What is making you hesitate?
2. Think about a season of pruning in your own life. What did it produce that comfort never could have?
3. What is the difference in your life between doing it alone and doing it along with God? Where do you feel that difference most?
4. God shows you the problem, and He has the provision — but what is the middle part that He is asking you to trust Him through right now?
5. What would it look like to stop treating hard as the ending and start treating it as the beginning? What is the first step forward that hard has been asking you to take?

HOWEVER,

The Painful Process of Pruning

Chapter 2

"The Power of Yet!"

A paperclip changed everything

He walked into my classroom in 5th grade with the worst handwriting I had ever seen. Not messy. Not rushed. Truly unreadable. Not by his classmates. Not by his mother. Not even by me.

And he had opinions about it.

Strong ones.

We fought. More than once. I made him rewrite papers he didn't want to rewrite. He pushed back the way children push back when they have been made to feel like the problem for too long. When every correction feels like confirmation that something is fundamentally wrong with them.

I could have put a period on him right there.

A lot of people already had.

But something made me stop one day and actually look. Not at the behavior. Not at the attitude. Not at the stack of illegible papers on my desk. I looked at the writing itself. Really looked. And I noticed something that changed everything.

His words ran together.

That was it. That was the whole problem. Not ability. Not effort. Not intelligence. Nobody had ever taught him how to put space between his words.

I found the smallest paperclip I could, and I sat down beside him. I showed him how to place it after each word before writing the next one. A simple tool. A simple technique. One nobody had ever bothered to show him before.

The next assignment he turned in — I didn't send it back.

When his mother saw it she cried.

She kept that paper for the longest time.

Because that paper wasn't just a legible assignment. That paper was proof that her son was not the problem. That he was not broken. That he had not been failing — he had simply been missing one small thing that nobody had ever thought to give him.

A paperclip.

And permission to not know something **yet.**

The period versus the ellipsis

I want to talk to you about punctuation for a moment.

Stay with me.

There are two ways to end an incomplete sentence. And the one you choose changes everything about what happens next.

I can't do it.

Read that again. Feel the weight of it. The finality. The door closing. The period sitting at the end like a stone — heavy, immovable, permanent. I can't do it, says this is who I am. This is where I stop. This is the boundary of what is possible for me.

Period.

Now read this —

I can't do it yet...

Feel the difference. The ellipsis at the end is not weakness. It is not avoidance. It is not pretending the struggle isn't real. The struggle is real. The limitation is real. The difficulty is completely acknowledged.

But the door is still open.

Yet says I am not finished becoming. Yet says this is where I am right now, not where I will always be. Yet says the paperclip is coming — I just haven't found it yet. Yet says hard is not the ending. Yet says —

Keep going.

The period is final. The yet is faithful.

And the most important thing I ever did as a teacher was refuse to let my students pick up a period when an ellipsis was still available to them.

The phone call

Five years passed.

That little boy became a young man. He moved through middle school and into high school. Life kept moving the way life does.

And then one day my phone rang.

It was him.

He wasn't calling his geometry teacher. He wasn't calling a tutor or a classmate or anyone else who might have been the logical choice. He was calling the teacher who found the paperclip. The teacher who marched up to that office when his mother came to take him home after a consequence and said —

No ma'am. He needs to feel this. He did the crime, he is doing the time.

The teacher who walked back to that cafeteria and looked him in the eye and said —

Your mom was here, and now she is gone. You are not going home today, buddy. Sit with this and feel all of it.

He called me because geometry was hard, and somewhere in him — underneath five years of growing up and moving on — he still remembered what I had taught him.

Hard doesn't mean stop.

You just haven't figured it out **yet.**

That phone call was not about geometry.

That phone call was a young man choosing an ellipsis over a period.

And I will never forget it as long as I live.

Yet is a lifestyle

I need to be honest with you about something.

The power of yet is not just something I taught my students. It is something I have had to live. Repeatedly. In seasons that had nothing to do with a classroom.

I went back to school during my divorce. While raising a son with severe asthma, who kept me in a constant state of alert. While navigating a daughter who was unraveling in ways that broke my heart daily. While managing with little to no family support underneath me.

Anyone looking at that season from the outside could have handed me a period and called it reasonable.

This is not the right time. Wait until things settle down. You can't do this right now.

But here is the truth about how I think.

I don't think about stop.

I think about — *I need to get this done and move on.*

That is not superhuman strength. That is not me being tougher than everyone else. That is simply what happens when you have decided — somewhere deep and early and permanent — that a period is not a punctuation mark you are willing to pick up.

Yet is not something I motivate myself with.

Yet is just how I see the world.

And I believe it is available to every single person reading this page right now.

Including you.

The only thing that can stop you is you

I told my students this from the very beginning.

The only thing that can stop you is you.

Not the hard. Not the struggle. Not the limitation. Not the season. Not the people who didn't show up for you. Not the teacher who never found your paperclip. Not the circumstances that were not your fault and not your choice.

Only you.

Because you are the one who decides which punctuation mark to pick up.

The period says I am done. The yet says I am still in process.

And being in process is not weakness. Being in process is not failure. Being in process is not something to be ashamed of or hidden or apologized for.

Being in process means you are still becoming.

And still becoming is the most powerful place a human being can live.

Yet and hard are best friends

Before we close this chapter, I want to connect something for you.

In Chapter 1 we talked about hard. About how hard is not the ending of your story but the beginning of the next chapter. About how the pruning — as painful as it is — is what produces the bloom.

Yet and hard work together. They are best friends. Two sides of the same coin.

Hard tells you what to **do** when things get difficult. Yet tells you what to **believe** about yourself while you are doing it.

Hard says — *do it anyway.* Yet says — *you can. You just haven't. Yet.*

You need both.

Hard without yet becomes grinding. Pushing through without believing it will ever produce anything.

Yet without hard becomes wishful thinking. Believing things will change without being willing to do the work.

But together?

Together they become the most powerful combination available to a human being navigating a difficult season.

Do it anyway. You can. You just haven't. Yet.

Prayer for Yet

Lord, thank you for the ellipsis. Thank you for the reminder that I am still in process and that being in process is exactly where You need me to be. On the days when the period looks like the easier choice — remind me that You are not finished with me yet. Give me eyes to see the paperclip solutions I have been missing. Give me the courage to sit with the hard long enough to find them. And let me be the person in someone else's life who refuses to put a period on them when You have written an ellipsis over their story. Amen.

Questions for reflection

1. Where in your life right now have you picked up a period that was never yours to carry? What would it look like to trade it for a yet?

2. Think about someone in your life — a child, a student, a friend, a colleague — who needs someone to find their paperclip. What have you been missing about their struggle that a closer look might reveal?

3. What is the difference between a period and
   an ellipsis in your own story right now?
   Where is God writing yet over something you
   have been calling finished?

4. The young man called five years later because
   he remembered what he had been taught.
   Who in your life is still carrying something
   you poured into them? How does that change
   the way you see your influence?

5. What would your life look like if you adopted
   yet as a lifestyle rather than an occasional
   encouragement? What periods would you
   have to be willing to put down?

HOWEVER,

The Painful Process of Pruning

Chapter 3

"The fear of doing is bigger than the actual doing."

The Saying

The fear of doing is bigger than the actual doing.

Read that again.

Not because it is complicated. Because it is true. And truth sometimes needs a second look before it settles.

The Story

I have proven this saying more times than I can count. It was not born from one moment. It was born from a pattern. A long, consistent, sometimes exhausting pattern of dreading something — and then doing it — and then looking back at the fear and thinking — *that was it? That was what had stopped me?*

The documentation I put off for weeks took two hours once I sat down. Conversations I rehearsed in my head for days that went better than anything I had imagined. Mountains that the fear built up into something unclimbable — that I climbed anyway — and found out they were hills.

The fear is a liar. Not always a loud one. Sometimes it is quiet. Sometimes it just sits between you and the thing you need to do and makes itself comfortable. Puts its feet up. Collects rent. And you let it — not because you are weak — but because the fear feels so much bigger than you in that moment that moving feels impossible.

I know that feeling. I know it well.

There was a season — not one day, not one moment, but a whole season — where life itself felt like it wanted to stop. The kind of hard that does not announce itself with one problem. It arrives with several. All at once. Divorce. Children who needed more than one person could reasonably give. Little to no support from the people who were supposed to show up. Bills. Decisions. Getting up anyway. Going to work anyway. Being mama anyway. Being a student anyway. Being still standing anyway.

The fear in that season was not the ordinary kind. It was not the fear of a hard conversation or a pile of paperwork. It was deeper than that. It was the fear of *what if I don't make it through this*. What if this is the thing that finally breaks me?

And I kept going.

Not because the fear went away. Not because I found some formula that made it smaller. Not because someone showed up with the right words at the right time. I kept going because I did not have a choice. I could not submit to the fear. Submitting was not an option I was willing to take.

So I built a bridge.

That is what I used to tell my kids when something hard was sitting in front of them. Start building a bridge to get over it. Some days, you will build it almost all the way and feel the other side getting close. Some days it will come completely down, and you will have to start from the beginning with nothing but the memory of what you already built. But if you keep going — if you refuse to let the coming down be the end of the building — one day the very thing you were building the bridge over will become the thing that carries you through the next time.

But I want to be honest with you about something.

I could not tell my children to build a bridge while I was still walking in the water. I had to build it first. I had to prove to myself that it could be done before I could hand that truth to anyone else — including the two people who needed it most from me. The bridge I was telling them to build — I was building mine at the same time. In the same hard seasons. With the same tired hands.

That is not a contradiction. That is just the truth of doing hard things in real time while other people are watching and needing you.

Did the bridge come down? Yes. More than once.
Did I have to start over? Yes. More than once. Did
the fear slow me down?

Yes. It slowed me down.

But a pause is not a stop. A pause is not yet.

I proved this saying again recently. More recently
than I would like to admit. I had work that had been
sitting. Months of it. The kind of pile that grows in
the corner of your mind and gets heavier every time
you look at it. And I looked at it. And I dreaded it.
And I let the fear collect its rent. Month after month.

Then an email came. And suddenly the work had to
get done. Not eventually. Now.

So I sat down. And I did it. In one month. While still
running my businesses. While still living my life.
While still being everything I am required to be to
everyone who needs me.

One month.

The fear had been living in my house for nine
months. The doing took one.

That is not a coincidence. That is the pattern. That is
the proof. The fear of doing is always — *always* —
bigger than the actual doing.

The Meaning

Fear is not your enemy. Let me be clear about that.
Fear is information. It tells you that something

matters. It tells you that the stakes are real. It tells you that you are human.

But fear was never meant to be your landlord.

When fear moves from information to occupation — when it stops telling you something and starts *running* something — that is when you have a problem. That is when the pile grows. That is when the months pass. That is when the thing that would have taken two hours sits for nine months because the fear convinced you it would take forever.

The fear of doing is bigger than the actual doing. Every time. Not some of the time. Every time.

Because the fear lives in your imagination. And your imagination has no limits. It can build that mountain as high as it wants to. It can make that conversation as catastrophic as it chooses. It can turn two hours of work into an insurmountable obstacle that you carry around like a weight for months.

The doing lives in reality. And reality has edges. Reality has an end. Reality can be finished.

Your imagination cannot be finished. The fear you build in your mind has no finish line. The actual doing always does.

And here is the part nobody tells you about the bridge.

The thing you build the bridge over does not disappear once you cross it. It transforms. The hard that almost broke you becomes the foundation that holds the next version of you steady. The divorce you survived becomes the strength you stand on when the next hard thing arrives. The season you were not sure you would make it through becomes the proof you pull out when the fear says *you won't make it through this either.*

You built the bridge. And now the bridge is holding you.

That is not motivation. That is architecture. That is what God does with the hard things we survive. He does not waste them. He builds with them.

Live It Out

Think about the thing you have been avoiding. You know what it is. You did not need me to tell you to think about it — it came to mind the moment I said it. That thing.

How long has the fear been collecting rent?

Now ask yourself honestly — if you sat down today and did it — how long would it actually take? Not how long the fear says it will take. How long it would *actually* take?

There is a gap between those two numbers. That gap is where the fear lives. That gap is what is costing you.

Now think about the bridge.

What are you building over right now? And is the bridge still standing, or did it come down recently, and you are sitting in the rubble trying to decide if it is worth starting again?

It is worth it. Start again.

You do not have to feel brave to begin. You do not have to have the whole bridge planned out before you lay the first board. You just have to start. One plank. One prayer. One day.

And if the bridge comes down — and sometimes it will — remember that starting over is not the same as starting from nothing. You carry everything you already built inside you. The fear does not get to take that.

And if you have to pause — pause. Rest if you need to. Breathe if you need to. Hold on if you need to.

But remember — a pause is not a stop. A pause is not yet.

Yet is still coming. And so is the other side of that bridge.

A Prayer for the Builder

Lord, the fear is real, and I am not going to pretend it isn't. But I know that You did not give me a spirit of fear. You gave me power. You gave me love. You gave me a sound mind. Help me to act like I believe that today. Help me to pick up what I need to pick up and start building. And when the bridge comes down — because sometimes it will — remind me

---

Discussion Questions

1. What is something you have been avoiding that the fear has made feel much larger than it probably is? How long has the fear been collecting rent on that space in your mind?
2. Think about the bridge. What is something hard in your past that you built a bridge over — that is now carrying you through something new? How does that change the way you see what you are currently going through?
3. Rhondnita says she could not tell her children to build a bridge while she was still walking in the water. Is there something you are trying to teach or give to someone else that you have not yet lived yourself? What would it look like to build it first?
4. The fear lives in imagination and has no limits. The doing lives in reality and has an end. How does that distinction change the way you think about the thing you are currently avoiding?

5. A pause is not a stop. A pause is not yet. Have you been calling a pause a stop in your own life? What would change if you renamed it?

The fear will always tell you the mountain is higher than it is and the water is deeper than it is and the bridge is impossible to build. Start building anyway. And if it comes down — start again. Because one day, the very thing you were trying to get over will be the thing that carries you. However, keep building.

HOWEVER,

The Painful Process of Pruning

Chapter 4

"I can't tell my kids to do hard things if I never do them myself."

The Saying

I can't tell my kids to do hard things if I never do them myself.

That is not a parenting philosophy. That is an integrity statement. And it costs something to say it.

The Story

It was a Monday. Not a designated hard day. Not a day set aside for processing or reflecting or feeling. It was a regular Monday in the middle of a pile of work that needed to get done. Notes to catch up. Businesses to run. Life happening the way life does — without asking if you are ready for it.

I put something on in the background. Something to fill the silence while I worked. And somewhere in the middle of all of it — without warning, without permission, without a single announcement — the tears came.

Just fell.

And I sat there for a moment trying to figure out where they came from. Because that is what I do. I am a processor. I need time to understand what is happening inside me before I can name it. And when I sat with it long enough to name it I realized — this was not one grief. This was all of them. At once. Finally showing up because they had been waiting too long for a proper place to land.

My son in law's birthday was coming. Gone too soon. And his birthday on the calendar felt like a door I was not sure I was ready to open. Underneath that was my Auntie. Grief I had not finished. And underneath that was Grandma Georgia — my safe place, my strong place, my foundation — and the goodbye I never got to say properly at her graveside because of an injury that kept me away. And underneath all of that was the loss of my grandmother and my father in law — a week apart. Him first. Then her. Grief stacked on grief with no room to breathe between them.

None of it had been properly sorted. Because life does not stop for sorting. Life just keeps going and you keep going with it and you put the grief somewhere you can function and you tell yourself you will deal with it later and later becomes months and months becomes a Monday with a video and tears that fall without asking first.

And I had a choice in that moment.

I could close the laptop. Push it back down. Get back to the notes. File it under later the way I had filed all the rest of it. Nobody would have known. Nobody was watching. It was just me and the grief and the Monday.

But the educator in me showed up. The part of me that has spent her life standing in front of people — in classrooms, in her home, in everything she has built — and telling them that hard things are survivable. That you do not run from the hard. That you build the bridge. That you keep going.

And she said — quietly, plainly, the way truth usually arrives —

You cannot teach courage while avoiding your own hard things.

I could not tell my kids to sit with hard things if I was quietly running from mine. I could not stand in front of a classroom and talk about resilience and doing hard things and getting through it — and then slip out the back door when my own hard thing showed up on a Monday afternoon.

That is not who I am. And it is not who I am willing to become.

So I stayed. I let the tears fall. I let the grief be what it was — messy and layered and long overdue. I did not perform it. I did not document it. I did not make it neat. I just stayed in it long enough to honor every single loss that showed up that Monday.

My son-in-law. My Auntie. Grandma Georgia. The goodbye I never got at the graveside. My grandmother and father in law a week apart.

I stayed for all of them.

And somewhere in the staying — in the refusing to run — this saying was born.

I can't tell my kids to do hard things if I never do them myself.

The Meaning

There is a word for teaching something you are not living. And that word is hypocrisy. And Rhondnita does not do hypocrisy.

I learned a long time ago not to sugarcoat or hide who I truly am. I am me, and I am okay with her. Flaws and all. And part of being okay with her is holding her accountable. Not just to the people she leads and teaches and raises. To herself.

Because here is what I know about children. They do not hear what you say nearly as loudly as they see what you do. You can give the most beautiful speech about courage and resilience and doing hard things — and if they watch you run from yours, they will remember the running. Not the speech.

Your life is the loudest lesson you will ever teach.

And it is not just children who are watching. It is everyone in your circle. Your students. Your colleagues. The women who look at you and think — if she can do it, maybe I can too. Every single one of them is reading your life more carefully than they are reading your words.

That is a weight. I will not pretend it isn't. There are days when the last thing you want is to be someone's example. There are days when you want to just be the one who gets to fall apart without it meaning something to somebody else.

But here is the other side of that weight.

The hard things you do — the griefs you stay with, the fears you face, the bridges you build and rebuild — they do not just carry you. They carry the people who are watching you. Every time you do the hard thing, you give someone else permission to do theirs. Every time you stay when you want to run, you show someone else that staying is possible.

You are not just doing it for you. You never were.

But — and this matters — you have to do it for you first. You cannot grieve for an audience. You cannot do hard things as a performance. The doing has to be real. It has to cost something. It has to be yours.

Do it for you first. Let it be real first. And then let it be the thing that gives someone else permission.

Live It Out

Think about the hard thing you have been avoiding. Not the task — we covered that in Chapter 3. This time I am asking about the emotional hard thing. The grief you filed under later. The feeling you closed the laptop on. The Monday you pushed through without stopping to honor what was sitting right there in front of you.

Who is watching you avoid it?

I am not asking that to shame you. I am asking it because sometimes the most powerful reason to do the hard thing is not for yourself. Sometimes you need a bigger reason to stay when everything in you wants to run. And if your children — or your students, or the people who look to you — are watching, let that be the reason that holds you in place long enough to start.

And then do it for real. Not for them. For you. Let the tears fall without asking permission. Let the grief be messy and layered and long overdue. Let the hard thing be exactly as hard as it actually is.

You cannot hand someone a bridge you have never built. You cannot teach someone to sit with grief you are still running from. The doing has to be yours first.

Always yours first.

A Prayer for the One Who Is Also Still Learning

Lord, I have been telling people to do hard things while quietly avoiding some of my own. You already know which ones. Help me to stop running. Help me to stay in the Monday when the tears come without warning, and the grief shows up uninvited, and the hard thing I have been filing under later finally arrives. Remind me that I cannot pour from a place I have never been. Remind me that the most important lesson I will ever teach is the one written in how I actually live. Help me to live it honestly. Flaws and all. Amen.

Discussion Questions

1. Is there a grief or a hard emotional thing you have been filing under later — pushing down, closing the laptop on, promising yourself you will deal with eventually? What would it look like to stay with it instead of running from it?

2. Rhondnita says your life is the loudest lesson you will ever teach. Who is watching your life right now? And what are they learning from what they see — not what they hear?

3. Think about a time someone in your life did a hard thing honestly — not perfectly, not without tears, but honestly. How did watching them do it affect your own ability to face something hard? Who might need to see you do the same?

4. There is a difference between doing hard things for an audience and doing them for real. How do you know the difference in your own life? What does it feel like when the doing is genuine versus performative?

5. Rhondnita says you have to do it for yourself first — and then let it be the thing that gives someone else permission. What hard thing, if you did it honestly and for real, might give

someone who is watching you permission to do theirs?

You have been telling people to do hard things. You have been building bridges and teaching courage and showing up for everyone who needs you. Now stay for your own Monday. Let the tears fall. Let the grief be what it is. Do the hard thing you have been avoiding — not for the audience, not for the lesson, but for you. Because you cannot give away what you have never lived. And because the most important however, in your story is the one you write with your own life. However, do it for real.

Part Two:

Faith as the Foundation

Breathe.

You just did something hard. You looked Part 1 in the eye — the doing of hard things, the power of yet, the fear that is bigger in your head than it ever is in the actual doing — and you did not put the book down. That matters. Take one breath and let it matter.

Now here is what Rhondnita is not going to tell you.

She is not going to tell you it gets easier from here. She is not going to tell you the hard is behind you or that the next pages are going to feel lighter than the ones you just came through. She does not deal in false hope, and she is not about to start.

What she is going to tell you is this.

You have not been moving alone. Not in Part One. Not before you picked up this book. Not in any hard season you have ever walked through. You thought you were doing it alone — most of us do — but there is a difference between alone and along. One letter. Everything.

Alone is your strength carrying the weight by itself.

Along is God's strength added to yours. His presence going before you into the hard. His provision already waiting on the other side of your obedience. His faithfulness seeing you through what He brought you to. His glory — not yours — being the point of the whole thing.

Part One said get up. Get moving. Do the hard thing.

Part Two shows you who has been moving with you all along.

This is not a breather from the hard. This is a chance to lift your eyes long enough to see who is walking beside you before you take the next step.

Along. Not alone.

Now keep going.

HOWEVER,

The Painful Process of Pruning

Chapter 5
"Godfidence"

The Saying
Godfidence.

Where It Came From

Rhondnita didn't coin this word.

She heard it somewhere — and stopped.

Not because it was new. Because it was already her. Because someone had finally put a name on something she had been living for years without knowing what to call it. That is the thing about the right word. It doesn't introduce you to something foreign. It introduces you to yourself.

She claimed it immediately. Not out of arrogance. Not because she had it all together or had figured out some secret that the rest of the world was missing. She claimed it because it described the only way she knew how to move — forward, in spite of everything trying to hold her back. With God as the foundation under every step.

That's Godfidence.

What It Means

The world has a version of confidence it likes to sell.

It looks polished. It sounds certain. It walks into rooms like it has never once questioned itself, never lost sleep, never sat in a truck on a long drive home wondering if it was enough. The world's version of confidence is the absence of doubt. The absence of struggle. The absence of the hard.

Rhondnita is not selling that version. She doesn't have it. And honestly — she doesn't want it.

Because Godfidence is something different entirely.

Godfidence is not the absence of struggle or doubt. It is the ability to move forward despite them.

Read that again slowly.

Despite them. Not after they are gone. Not once they quiet down. Not when the fear finally lifts and the path gets clear and everything lines up neatly on both sides. Despite. While they are still present. While the doubt is still loud. While the hard is still hard.

That is what walking in who God made you actually looks like from the inside. It does not feel like certainty every morning. Some mornings it feels like lacing up your shoes when you don't want to and walking out the door anyway. Some mornings it feels like sitting in a truck asking God if you heard

Him right. Some mornings it feels like shaking —
and going anyway.

The going anyway. That is Godfidence.

Warmth and steel at the same time. Grace and
power occupying the same body simultaneously. Not
one or the other. Both. Because God did not make
Rhondnita soft or strong. He made her soft and
strong. The tenderness that loves her students
fiercely and the steel that gets up after betrayal —
that is not a contradiction. That is the whole point.

People see it on her before she says a word. There is
something in the way she walks into a room — not
like she owns it, but like she belongs in it. Like she
was sent there. Like whatever comes next, she will
still be standing when it is over. Not because
nothing touches her. Because she has decided that
nothing will stop her.

That decision — that is the Godfidence they are
seeing.

The Testimony Behind It

Here is what Godfidence has looked like in
Rhondnita's actual life. Not in theory. In practice.

It looked like three degrees completed despite a
divorce — while raising two children, largely alone,
with little to no support from the people who should
have shown up. Nobody was handing her extra
hours in the day. Nobody was making it easier. She
moved forward anyway.

It looked like a fourth degree in 2023, while running a business she had built from the ground up in the middle of a global pandemic. She moved forward anyway.

It looked like walking into rooms where she was the only one who looked like her, who had come from where she came from, who had carried what she had carried — and not shrinking. Not apologizing. Not making herself smaller so others could be more comfortable. She moved forward anyway.

It looked like sitting in hard seasons — grief layered on grief, loss stacked on loss — and still getting up. Still showing up for her students. Still running her businesses. Still choosing to finish this book when finishing things has never come easy.

Moving forward anyway.

That is not arrogance. That is not performance. That is not someone who never doubted or never struggled or never sat in the truck wondering if she was enough.

That is a woman who decided the doubt did not get to drive.

God gets to drive. She gets to ride forward.

Live It Out

Godfidence does not arrive one day fully formed. It is built. It is built in the moments you choose to move when everything in you wants to stop.

So here is the practice:

When the doubt shows up — and it will — name it. Don't pretend it isn't there. Rhondnita is not about pretending. Acknowledge it. I see you. I feel you. And I am moving anyway.

Find the one next step. Not the whole staircase. Not the final destination. The one next step that Godfidence looks like right now, in this moment. Take it. That is the whole assignment for today.

Remember that Godfidence is not your strength alone. It is God's strength added to yours. That is the difference between going alone and going along. One letter. Everything.

And when you walk into the room — whatever room that is for you — walk in like you were sent there. Because you were.

Prayer

Lord, you did not promise me easy. You promised me You. And You have been there in every hard season, every doubt, every moment I wanted to stop. Today I choose to move forward — not because I have it figured out, but because You do. Let my moving forward be the evidence. Let Godfidence be visible. Not so people see me — but so they see what You can do with a willing woman who refuses to quit. Amen.

Discussion Questions

1. How have you defined confidence in the past? How does Godfidence challenge or expand that definition for you?

2. Think about a time you moved forward despite doubt or struggle. What did that cost you — and what did it produce?

3. Rhondnita describes Godfidence as warmth wrapped in steel — power and grace at the same time. Which side of that comes more naturally to you? Which side do you need to lean into?

4. There is a difference between going alone and going along with God. Where in your life right now are you going alone when God is asking to go along?

5. What is the one room you need to walk into like you were sent there? What has been stopping you? What does Godfidence look like in that specific moment?

HOWEVER,

The Painful Process of Pruning

Chapter 6

"God's Will — God's Bill"

The Saying

God's will — God's bill.

Where It Came From

This saying did not come from a good season.

It came from the floor.

Rhondnita was going through her first and only divorce. The kids were on reduced lunch that year. Reduced lunch — and there were days she did not even have that. So every day, she and her children would walk through the house together looking for change. Couch cushions. Coat pockets. Counter tops. The bottom of a purse. Whatever was there. And every day — not most days, every day — they found just enough.

Not extra. Not a surplus. Not a sign that things were turning around. Just enough for that day. Just enough for the next morning's lunch money. Just enough to keep going one more day.

And then the next day they would do it again.

She thought about the story in 1 Kings 17. The widow of Zarephath. A woman at the absolute end of everything — enough flour and oil for one last meal, for herself and her son, and then it was over. That was her plan. Make the last meal. Eat it. Die. And then Elijah showed up and asked her to make his first.

She obeyed. And the jar did not run out. The jug did not run dry. Not once. Not until the drought was over.

Rhondnita was that woman. Walking the floors of her house, finding change in the forgotten corners, feeding her children on what should not have been enough — and watching it be enough anyway. Every single day.

That is where this saying was born. Not in abundance. In the walking. In the trusting, when trusting was the only option she had left.

God's will. God's bill.

If He assigns it — He funds it. You don't have to figure out the how.

What It Means

The world has a process for doing things.

You make a plan. You save the money. You build the foundation. You wait until the conditions are right and the timing makes sense and the risk is manageable and everyone who loves you thinks it is a good idea. Then — maybe — you move.

God's process does not always look like that.

Sometimes God's process looks like a resignation letter with no safety net. Sometimes it looks like change found on the floor of a house where things are tight and the future is unclear and you are raising two children largely alone and nobody is coming to make it easier. Sometimes it looks like stepping out before you can see where your foot is going to land.

And somehow — the floor is there.

That is the thing about God's will. It does not come with a detailed budget breakdown and a five-year projection. It comes with a call. A tug. A voice that gets quieter the longer you ignore it and louder the longer you stay put. And when you finally move — when you finally say yes to the thing He has been asking you to do — the provision shows up. Not always early. Not always in the way you expected. But it shows up.

Because God does not assign what He has not already funded. He does not call you to something and then abandon you in the middle of it. He is not that kind of God. He is the jar that doesn't run out. The change that is always just enough. The resignation that lands two weeks before the whole world shuts down.

He is never late. He is just rarely early enough to satisfy our anxiety.

The Testimony Behind It

In 2017, Rhondnita told her principal she was not feeling the classroom anymore. Her principal told her about the time she herself had left education and came back within six months. Rhondnita stayed.

Then she got sick. She stayed another year.

Then her principal left, and the school got a new one. And this one called her into his office and told her she was a bad teacher, because children who had been handed to her already behind, already struggling, already carrying more than children should carry, had not hit a benchmark on a state test.

She sat in that office and heard something else entirely.

Are you going to leave — or am I going to have to make you leave?

She put her resignation in.

Two weeks later, COVID-19 shut down the world. Every school. Every classroom. Every door that had felt like the safe and stable option closed simultaneously — and Rhondnita had already walked through hers.

She did not have a perfect plan. She did not have a fully funded business model. She had a resignation, a calling that had been tugging at her since 2017, and a God who had already been paying bills she didn't know were due yet.

The 2020 business was not a hey, let's start a business kind of thing. It was an act of obedience. It was a woman finally saying yes to the thing God had been asking her to do — and watching Him cover what she could not cover herself.

That is God's will. That is God's bill.

This saying got buried for a while. The years between 2022 and now were heavy. Grief layered on grief. Loss stacked on loss. There are seasons where even the truest things you know get quiet under the weight of what you are carrying. That is not failure. That is being human in a hard season.

But the saying came back. It resurfaced during this journey — this book, this writing, this finally finishing something. And when it came back it came back with more weight behind it than it had before. Because now Rhondnita knows something she could not have known in the divorce season or the resignation season.

It has always been true. Every single time. The jar has never run out.

Live It Out

What is the thing God has been tugging at you to do?

Not a comfortable thing. Not the thing that makes sense on paper and gets nods of approval from everyone around you. The specific thing. The one that has been in the background of your life for longer than you want to admit. The one you have stayed put on — busy, productive, accomplished in other areas — but stayed put on.

Name it. Write it down if you need to.

Now ask yourself honestly — have you been waiting for the bill to make sense before you agreed to the will? Have you been asking God to show you the full budget before you take the first step?

Here is what Rhondnita knows from the floors of that house and the resignation letter and the business built in the middle of a pandemic:

The bill does not always show up before the will requires your yes. Sometimes the provision is on the other side of the obedience. Sometimes the jar doesn't fill until you pick it up and start pouring.

You don't have to figure out the how. That was never your assignment. Your assignment is the yes.

God's will. God's bill.

Trust the one who has never once let the jar run out.

Prayer

Lord, you have been faithful in every season — even the ones where I could not see it clearly until I looked back. You covered what I could not cover.

You funded what I could not fund. You showed up in couch cushion change, in the timing of a resignation, and in a business born from obedience. Today I choose to trust the will even when I cannot see the bill. Increase my faith where my fear is loudest. And remind me — when I forget — that the jar has never run out. Not once. Amen.

Discussion Questions

1. Has there been a season in your life where God's provision showed up as just enough — not extra, not early, but exactly enough? What did that teach you about His faithfulness?

2. Where in your life right now are you waiting for the bill to make sense before you say yes to the will? What would it look like to take the first step before the full provision is visible?

3. Rhondnita heard God ask her — Are you going to leave or am I going to have to make you leave? Have you ever felt God nudging you toward something you kept putting off? What finally moved you — or what is still keeping you in place?

4. The widow of Zarephath obeyed before she had evidence the jar would last. Where do you need that kind of obedience right now? What is your make his first moment?

5. This saying got buried under heavy seasons
    and resurfaced during a journey toward
    finishing something important. What truth in
    your own life has gotten quiet under the
    weight of hard years — and what would it
    mean to let it surface again?

HOWEVER,

The Painful Process of Pruning

Chapter 7

"If God Brings You To It — He Will See You Through It"

The Saying

If God brings you to it — He will see you through it.

Where It Came From

This one did not come from a single moment.

It came from a life.

There was a church. Not the church Rhondnita grew up in — the one where her grandmother and her mother sat in the same pews and faith was passed down like a family recipe. This was a different church. The one she ran to when her first marriage fell apart and she felt completely alone. The one where she came back to God — not the God she had inherited, but the God she chose. Her own. Personal. Real.

She rededicated her life to Christ in that building. Started living honestly for Him in that building. And somewhere in the middle of all of that — in the middle of the rebuilding, the relearning, the becoming — a young woman said something to her that she was not ready to hear.

Just one sentence.

Get to know God for yourself.

Rhondnita hung up the phone.

Not because the sentence was wrong. Because the sentence was right — and she was in too much pain for right to feel good. She was in the middle of a divorce. The ground was shifting under her feet. The future was completely unclear. And this young woman had the nerve to say something true when what Rhondnita needed — or thought she needed — was someone to sit in the pain with her.

She was mad. She hung up.

And she never forgot a single word of it.

That is how God works sometimes. He does not wait for you to be in the right mood to receive what He has for you. He slips it in through a phone call that ends in frustration. Through a moment of anger. Through a sentence you are not ready for that takes root anyway — quietly, stubbornly — because the truth has a way of surviving even when we slam the door on it.

Years later, Rhondnita called that young woman back. Not to apologize exactly — but to thank her. For being courageous enough to give her what she needed, even when it was not what she wanted. For not softening the truth to make it easier to swallow. For saying the hard thing anyway.

It was the most important piece of advice Rhondnita had ever received. Or given.

Because she became that young woman for someone else. The chain did not stop with her. She passed the courage on. Gave someone else what they needed instead of what they wanted. Probably got hung up on too.

That is how God sees you through. Sometimes through a choir on a Sunday morning. Sometimes, through one sentence from one person on a phone call that ends before it should. Sometimes, through the very thing that made you mad enough to hang up.

He was already seeing her through before she knew what the through was going to cost.

What It Means

This saying is not a bumper sticker.

Rhondnita knows that because she has lived every word of it in ways that were not tidy or comfortable or easy to summarize.

The divorce. The degrees earned in the middle of it — three of them, while raising two children largely alone with little to no support from the people who should have shown up. The son with severe asthma and allergies, and every sleepless night that came with that. The daughter who tested every boundary she had. The abusive relationships. The betrayals. The court battles. The layered losses of 2022. Life in general — which for Rhondnita has never been a small or simple thing.

He brought her to every single one of those things.

And He saw her through every single one.

That is not a theological statement. That is a testimony. That is a woman looking back at the full length of her life and saying — the evidence is there. Every hard thing. Every impossible season. Every moment where the other side was not visible and the through felt like too much to ask. He was there. He did not leave. The jar did not run out.

So when the next hard thing came — and it always came — she did not need a new miracle to believe. She just needed to remember the last one. And the one before that. And the one before that.

Faith built on evidence is the most solid kind there is.

If He brought me through that — He will bring me through this.

That is not a saying she picked up somewhere and decided sounded good. That is a conclusion she reached after years of watching God be faithful in seasons that had no business producing faithfulness. It is the quiet knowing. Not dramatic. Not loud. Just settled. Just sure.

Just always there.

The Testimony Behind It

There is a young woman Rhondnita has never forgotten.

She does not know if that woman remembers the conversation. She may not remember that Rhondnita hung up on her. But Rhondnita was standing in the middle of one of the hardest seasons of her life — marriage falling apart, ground shifting under her feet, the future completely unclear — and this woman looked past the pain and said six words that became the foundation of everything that came after.

Get to know God for yourself.

Not the God of your grandmother's church. Not the God of obligation or tradition or inherited faith. The God who is yours. Personal. Present. Real to you specifically.

Rhondnita hung up the phone.

She was not ready. The truth was too clean for how messy her life felt in that moment. The advice was too simple for how complicated the pain was. She needed someone to sit in it with her — not hand her a road map out of it.

But the sentence stayed. She could not shake it. And eventually — not that day, not that week, maybe not even that year — she started doing exactly that. Getting to know Him for herself. And what she found was a God who does not bring you to something and then disappear. A God who is not interested in your comfort as much as He is interested in your completion. A God who will see you through the divorce and the degrees and the sleepless nights and the courtrooms and the betrayals and the grief — not because the through is easy but because He said He would.

Years later, she called that young woman back and said thank you. Thank you for being courageous enough to give me what I needed, even when it was not what I wanted. Thank you for not softening it. Thank you for saying the hard thing anyway.

The young woman had given her the most important piece of advice she had ever received.

And Rhondnita made sure it did not stop there. She became that young woman for someone else. Passed the courage on. Said the hard thing when the easy thing would have been more comfortable. Gave what was needed instead of what was wanted.

Probably got hung up on too.

That is the through. That is what it looks like when God sees you all the way through something — not just to the other side of your own pain, but into the lives of the people behind you who are still in the middle of theirs.

Live It Out

Look back before you look forward.

This is not about living in the past. This is about building your faith on what is already true. Pull out your own evidence. The thing you did not think you were going to survive. The season that felt like it was going to be the one that finally broke you. The moment where the through felt impossible.

You are still here.

That means He saw you through it. That means the evidence is already in your possession. That means the next hard thing — whatever it is — does not get to tell you He won't come through. Because He already has. More times than you have probably stopped to count.

Find your phone call moment. The sentence someone said to you that made you want to hang up. The truth that landed wrong because the pain was too loud. Sit with it. Ask yourself honestly — was there something in it that took root anyway? Something that stayed even after you slammed the door on it?

And then ask yourself this — are you being that young woman for someone else? Are you courageous enough to give people what they need even when it is not what they want? Even when they might hang up on you?

That is the completion of the through. Not just surviving it yourself. Reaching back for the person still in the middle of it.

Prayer

Lord, thank you for the sentences I was not ready for. Thank you for the people courageous enough to say the hard thing when the easy thing would have been more comfortable. Thank you for letting truth take root even in the moments I slammed the door on it. And thank you for seeing me through every single thing you brought me to — not just to the other side of my own pain but into the lives of the people behind me who still need what you gave me. Make me courageous enough to pass it on. Even if they hang up. Amen.

Discussion Questions

1. Has someone ever said something true to you that you were not ready to hear? Did you hang up — literally or figuratively? What happened to that truth over time?

2. Rhondnita describes her faith in this saying as a quiet knowing — not dramatic, not loud, just always there. How would you describe the faith that has carried you through your hardest seasons?

3. Look back at your own life. What is the thing you did not think you were going to survive — and did? How does that evidence speak to what you are facing right now?

4. God deposits things in us before we know we will need them — a sentence, a song, a moment, a memory. What has He deposited

in you that you are still making withdrawals
from?

5. This saying pairs with God's will — God's bill.
   Together, they say He assigns it, He funds it,
   and He finishes it. Are you being that young
   woman for someone else right now? Are you
   courageous enough to give what is needed
   even when it is not what is wanted — even if
   they hang up?

HOWEVER,

The Painful Process of Pruning

Chapter 8

"Lord Decrease Me and Increase You — So People See More of You and Less of Me"

The Saying

Lord decrease me and increase you — so people see more of you and less of me.

Where It Came From

This one was a prayer before it was a saying.

Rhondnita used to pray it regularly. Not as a performance. Not as something that sounded good on a Sunday morning when everything was fine. As a daily conversation with God about who she wanted to be in the world — and who she wanted people to see when they looked at her.

Not her. Him. Through her.

It started with another prayer. The prayer of Jabez. 1 Chronicles 4:10. Jabez asked God to bless him and enlarge his territory. To keep His hand with him. To keep him from evil. It is a prayer of expansion. Of trust. Of asking God for more — more influence, more reach, more ground to stand on for His purposes.

Rhondnita prayed it. And somewhere in the praying of it she understood something that nobody had to teach her. Something she arrived at not in a classroom or a Bible study but in the living of her own life.

I can't expect Him to enlarge my territory if I am not willing to allow Him to decrease my flesh.

You cannot pray Jabez and skip the surrender. You cannot ask God to expand what you are not willing to empty. The enlargement requires the decrease. The blessing requires the surrender. The territory cannot grow if the flesh is still sitting in the middle of it taking up space.

So the Jabez prayer led her directly to John 3:30. He must increase, but I must decrease. John the Baptist said it about Jesus — at the height of his own ministry, with his own followers, his own reputation, his own moment — and he pointed everything away from himself and toward Christ. Not because he had nothing. Because he understood that the point was never him.

That is where the prayer came from. Not from a single moment of dramatic surrender. From the quiet conclusion of a woman reading scripture and recognizing herself in it. From understanding that you cannot have both — the spotlight and the vessel. You have to choose.

She chose the vessel.

It came easy in the knowing. She understood it the way you understand something that has already settled deep in you — the way you understand that a vessel has to be emptied before it can be filled. That dying to your flesh is the price of being used by God. She knew that. She accepted it. She meant it when she prayed it.

And then the cost came due.

Because knowing and doing are two entirely different transactions. The knowing was clean. The doing — the actual dying — that was the cost. Letting go of loved ones she did not want to release. Confronting things about herself she did not want to see. Walking through a season so heavy it buried this prayer along with everything else that required full surrender.

2022 deserves its own space, and it will have it. But its weight belongs here — not the details, the weight. Because that season did not just challenge Rhondnita. It forced her to confront herself. It cost her relationships. It cost her the comfortable version of who she thought she was. It stripped things away that she had not agreed to give up.

And somewhere in the middle of all of that stripping — in the grief and the letting go and the confronting — she found herself reaching for this prayer again. Not dramatically. Not all at once. It just started coming back. The way things come back when you have been away from them long enough to understand what they were holding for you.

Lord, decrease me and increase you.

It was not just humility this time. It was survival. It was a woman finding her way back to herself — not the self that needed to be seen, but the self that was willing to be used. Not the spotlight. The vessel.

And underneath it all — underneath the decrease and the increase and the dying to flesh — was the prayer beneath the prayer. The one that had always been there. The one that made all the costs make sense.

Lord, don't let this pain be in vain.

Take it. All of it. The divorce and the degrees and the sleepless nights and the betrayals and the letting go and the confronting and the 2022 weight. Take all of it and use it. Don't let it be wasted. Let someone see You in what I survived.

That is not humility. That is consecration.

What It Means

There is a scripture that says they overcame by the blood of the Lamb and by the word of their testimony. Revelation 12:11. Rhondnita knows that verse. She had to learn to believe it about herself.

Because a testimony is only powerful when you believe it. When you stop looking at what everyone else survived and start owning what you survived. When you stop diminishing your own story because it doesn't look like someone else's. When you look in the mirror and say — that happened. I walked through that. God saw me through that. And it is not just my story. It is someone else's way through.

Rhondnita had to start believing her own testimony.

That is what decrease me and increase you really means in the deep places. It is not self-erasure. It is reorientation. It is the decision that the story of her life — the divorce, the degrees, the children raised largely alone, the businesses built from obedience, the grief, the letting go, the surviving of things that had no business being survivable — does not belong to her ego. It belongs to God's glory. And to whoever needs to hear it to keep going.

A vessel. Not a spotlight.

The spotlight wants credit. The spotlight needs to be seen. The spotlight makes the story about the one who survived.

The vessel wants something different entirely. The vessel says — look what God can carry. Look what He can do with a willing woman who keeps showing up even when the dying costs everything. Look what He can pour through someone who has been emptied enough times to know the emptying is not the end.

That is Godfidence without the ego. That is God's will without the personal agenda. That is the through — not just survived but surrendered.

You cannot ask God to enlarge your territory while your flesh is still sitting in the middle of it. The

Jabez prayer and the John 3:30 prayer are not two separate prayers. They are one complete act of faith. Ask for the enlargement. Accept the decrease. Trust that what God fills is always greater than what the flesh held.

Decrease me. Increase you.

So they see more of You and less of me.

The Testimony Behind It

Rhondnita is not a woman who needs a spotlight.

She will walk into a room like she was sent there — because she was. She will speak truth without apology — because someone needs it. She will finish this book — because someone is waiting for it. But none of that is for her name. None of that is for the applause or the platform or the recognition.

It is for the woman in the back of the room who came in on her last thread. The one who has been carrying something too heavy for too long and needs to know the comma is not the end. The one who needs to hear that someone else walked through the divorce and the degrees and the betrayal and the 2022 weight — and came out still standing. Still believing. Still willing to be used.

That woman is why Rhondnita prays decrease me.

Because if the story is about Rhondnita — it reaches only as far as Rhondnita's name can carry it. But if the story is about what God can do with a willing vessel — it reaches into places Rhondnita will never go. Into living rooms and hospital waiting rooms and trucks on long drives home and recliners where things finally settle. Into the hard middle of someone else's however.

That is the point of the pain. That is the answer to the prayer beneath the prayer.

Lord, don't let this pain be in vain.

He hasn't. He won't. He is using every bit of it — right now, through these pages, through this woman who finally decided to finish something.

The vessel is full. And it is pouring.

Live It Out

Start with the Jabez prayer. Ask God to bless you. To enlarge your territory. To keep His hand with you. Mean every word of it.

And then stay there long enough to hear what it requires.

Because the enlargement comes with a condition. Not a punishment — a preparation. You cannot hold more of God's blessing while your flesh is still occupying the space He needs to fill. The territory cannot expand while you are still standing in the middle of it protecting what is yours.

So pray the second prayer. *Lord, decrease me and increase you.* Let it cost what it costs. The dying is real. Rhondnita is not going to tell you otherwise.

But what comes after the dying — the being used, the testimony that becomes someone else's weapon, the pain that does not go to waste — that is worth every bit of what it cost.

And if you have a testimony you have been sitting on — start believing it. Not because it makes you look good. Because someone needs it to keep going. Your story is not just yours. It never was. It belongs to whoever needs it next.

Don't let your pain be in vain.

Pour it out. Let God use it. Be the vessel.

Prayer

Lord, I come to you first with the Jabez prayer — bless me, enlarge my territory, keep your hand with me. And then I stay long enough to hear what that requires. Decrease me. Increase you. So people see more of you and less of me. Take everything this life has cost — the hard seasons, the letting go, the confronting of things I did not want to see, the pain I carried longer than I should have had to. Take all of it and use it. Let it reach someone I will never meet. Let it hold someone up on a day I will never know about. I cannot ask you to enlarge what I am not willing to surrender. So here it is. All of it. Don't let this pain be in vain. Not one drop of it. Amen.

Discussion Questions

1. Rhondnita connected the Jabez prayer to John 3:30 — you cannot ask God to enlarge your territory if you are not willing to allow Him to decrease your flesh. Where in your own life are you praying for enlargement while holding onto something that needs to be surrendered first?

2. What is the difference between a vessel and a spotlight in your own life right now? Which one are you operating as most often — and what would it take to shift?

3. Rhondnita describes the decrease me prayer as easy in the knowing and costly in the doing. Where in your own life is there a surrender you understand in your head but have not yet made in your hands?

4. Rhondnita prays — Lord, don't let this pain be in vain. What pain in your own life are you still waiting to see used? What would it mean to release it into God's hands and trust Him with what it produces?

5. This chapter closes Part 2 — Faith as the Foundation. Looking at all four chapters together — Godfidence, God's will, God's bill, If He brings you to it, and Decrease me — which one speaks most directly to where you are right now? What is God saying to you through it?

HOWEVER,

The Painful Process of Pruning.

Part Three — Surviving the Hard Seasons

Maybe you picked up this book and skipped straight to this section because something in the title found you before you were ready to be found.

Maybe you did not even know you were looking for this page until you were already on it.

That is not an accident.

This section is for the woman who does not yet know she is surviving. The one who has been so busy holding everyone else together — absorbing everyone else's hard, carrying everyone else's weight, being the place everyone else dumps what they cannot carry themselves — that she has not stopped long enough to notice that she is still standing underneath all of it.

Still standing. Still breathing. Still showing up.

That is surviving. Even if it does not look like what you thought surviving was supposed to look like.

Surviving does not always look like strength. Sometimes it looks like not today. I will not stop today. Sometimes it looks like staring at a problem so big you cannot see around it, and breaking it down to the only size you can manage right now —

one breath. One minute. One hour. One day. Whatever size right now needs to be.

Sometimes surviving looks like smiling when every single thing inside of you wants to cry. Not because you are pretending. Because you have learned that the smile is sometimes the only thing between you and the wave. And you are choosing the smile. That is not weakness. That is a decision.

Sometimes surviving looks like giving yourself permission to bring God the most honest prayer you have ever prayed. Not a prayer of declaration. Not a prayer of warfare. Not a prayer that sounds like you have it all together. Just —

Lord. I'm here.

That is enough. That is a full prayer. That is a woman who showed up when she did not have to. When she could have stopped. When nobody would have blamed her if she had. And she showed up anyway and said — I'm here. And God can work with I'm here. He has been working with I'm here since the beginning of time.

Surviving is not sugarcoating what is happening. It is living despite of what is happening. Despite of. Not after. Not when it gets better. Not once the hard passes. Despite of. While the grief is still fresh. While the wave is still moving. While the weight is still heavy and the answer is still unclear and the path forward is still invisible.

Despite of is one of the most powerful places a person can live.

And here is what nobody tells the survivors. The ones who are still in it. The ones who have not yet reached the other side of the hard season they are currently inside of.

You are allowed to say I am drowning.

Not as a declaration of defeat. Not as a final word. Just as an honest one. I am drowning, and I just need a few minutes to come up for air. That is not giving up. That is a woman who knows herself well enough to know what she needs. That is wisdom wearing the face of vulnerability. That is strength doing the bravest thing strength can do — admitting it needs a moment.

Come up for air. Take the breath. Say the honest prayer. Break it down to the smallest size you can survive inside of.

The chapters in this section were not written from a comfortable distance. They were written from inside the hard. From grief seasons still active. From Mondays that carried more weight than one day should have to carry. From the exhaustion of being the strong one for so long that the idea of being weak for a moment felt like a luxury she could not afford.

They were written by a woman still surviving her own hard seasons who decided that the most honest thing she could do was tell the truth about what surviving actually looks like from the inside.

Not sugarcoated. Not polished. Not written from the other side.

Written from right here. Right now. Despite of.

If you are in a hard season right now — this section was written for you. Not for who you will be when you get through it. For who you are right now. In the middle of it. Still breathing. Still showing up. Still saying I'm here even when I'm here is the best you have got.

I'm here is enough.

You are enough.

Keep going.

HOWEVER,

The Painful Process of Pruning

Chapter 9

"One day at a time — One moment at a time — One prayer at a time."

There is a lie that hard seasons tell you. The lie is that you have to solve all of it. Right now. Today. Every problem, every wound, every unanswered question, every bill, every betrayal, every grief, every heavy thing sitting on your chest — all of it requiring your attention simultaneously, all of it demanding a solution you do not have yet.

That lie will exhaust you before the hard even finishes introducing itself.

Rhondnita knows this lie personally. She has heard it in more seasons than she can count. During the divorce that dismantled the life she thought she was building. During the nights her son's breathing became the only thing that mattered in the entire world. During the seasons her daughter was in a place that tested every boundary, every nerve, and every ounce of strength Rhondnita had — and she was navigating all of it largely alone, without the family support she needed, holding the line the best she knew how. During 2022 — and if you know, you know, and if you don't, just understand that 2022 was the kind of hard that threatened everything. Her family. Her closest friendship of nearly twenty years. Her career. Her freedom. All of it on the line at once. All of it built on a lie someone else told.

And then there was a day in March of 2026. Not ancient history. Not a season she is writing about from a comfortable distance. Recent. Raw. Professional pressures sitting on one side. The grief still fresh and layered on another. And the kind of quiet, heavy ache that can settle into your personal life and sit there — the kind the reader may know something about without Rhondnita having to say another word about it.

Everything coming at once. Again.

Because that is the thing nobody warns you about hard seasons. They do not take turns. They do not line up politely and wait for you to finish with one before the next one steps forward. They arrive together. All of them. At the same time. Loud and heavy and relentless.

And somewhere in the middle of all of that — Rhondnita remembered.

One day at a time.

And when that got too big — one hour.

And when that got too big — thirty minutes.

And when that got too big — five minutes.

And when that got too big — one minute.

And when that got too big — one breath.

Read that again. Not as a list. As a lifeline. As a woman dismantling time itself into pieces small enough to survive inside of. Because when you are in the throws of hard, you are not organizing your life. You are not making a plan. You are not thinking about next year or next month or next week. You are thinking about right now. This breath. This minute. This prayer.

One prayer at a time means you are not asking God to fix everything simultaneously. You are bringing Him one thing. The most pressing thing. The thing that is sitting on your chest at this exact moment. And you are trusting that He can handle the rest while you breathe through this one.

This saying has never left Rhondnita. It has just been rediscovered in each new season of hard. It was there during the divorce. It was there during the illness. It was there during the seasons that tested every boundary she had. It was there in 2022 when the ground beneath her shifted in ways she is still not ready to fully name on these pages. And it was there on a day in March of 2026 when everything came at once again, and God sent the reminder — stop trying to solve all of it. You were never supposed to carry all of it at once.

You were only ever supposed to carry right now.

Just this breath. Just this moment. Just this prayer.

That is not weakness. That is wisdom. That is a woman who has survived enough hard seasons to know that the only way through is through — and sometimes through looks like five minutes at a time.

Hard has been around for a long time in Rhondnita's life. But so has anyway. And so has one more breath. One more minute. One more prayer.

The hard did not win in 2022. It did not win during the divorce. It did not win during the illness or the challenging seasons or the betrayals or the professional pressures or the quiet heavy ache of that day in March. It has not won yet.

Because Rhondnita is still here. Still breathing. Still praying. Still going.

One day at a time. One moment at a time. One prayer at a time.

Live It Out

When everything feels like it is coming at once — and it will — resist the urge to solve all of it simultaneously. Ask yourself one question. What is the smallest unit of time I can manage right now? Start there. Not with the whole problem. Not with the whole season. Just with right now.

One day. One hour. Thirty minutes. Five minutes. One minute. One breath. Whatever size right now needs to be — start there. Bring God one prayer. The most pressing one. Trust Him with the rest.

A Prayer for Right Now

Lord, I cannot hold all of this at once. I was not built to. Remind me when I forget that You did not ask me to solve everything today. You asked me to trust You today. Help me break this down to a size I can breathe inside of. One moment. One prayer. One step. And when even that gets too big — one breath. I trust You with everything I cannot carry right now. Amen.

Discussion Questions

1. What hard season in your life required you to break time down into the smallest possible pieces just to survive it? What did that look like for you?

2. Rhondnita describes the lie that hard seasons tell — that you have to solve everything at once. Where have you heard that lie in your own life? How did it affect you?

3. What is the difference between breaking it down and giving up? How do you know when you are surviving versus surrendering?

4. Is there a season in your life so layered and heavy you are not ready to fully name it yet? What has carrying that season taught you about yourself?

5. What is the one prayer you need to bring to God right now? Not the whole list. Just the one that is sitting on your chest at this exact moment. Write it down.

HOWEVER,

The Painful Process of Pruning

Chapter 10

"Grief is like an ocean — it comes in waves and tides — but some days it is just still — I am thankful for the still days."

Nobody tells you that grief is not one thing.

They hand you a casserole and a sympathy card and they sit with you for a season and then life moves on for everyone except you. Because grief does not move on. Grief moves in. It unpacks its things quietly and it does not ask permission and it does not give you a timeline and it does not distinguish between the losses that come with funerals and the ones that don't.

Rhondnita knows this personally.

There are four seats at the table of her deepest losses. Grandma Georgia — her safe place, her strong place, her foundation. The woman who loved Rhondnita's lasagna so much she could not say the word correctly and called it cazagna instead. Rhondnita could not get to her graveside when she left this earth. That incompleteness sat in her chest for a long time — until a letter written during this very project became the real goodbye she never got to say. Aunt Shirley — named in the dedication of this book because some people deserve to have their name in print as a testament to what they poured into you. Her father in law. And her son-in-law — a private man who did not share his illness widely and whose privacy is honored here the same way it was honored in his living. He is not named on these pages. He does not need to be. Rhondnita knows who she is writing about. And so does God.

Four deaths. Four real and heavy and permanent losses.

But grief is not only death.

There are losses that do not come with casseroles or sympathy cards or anyone sitting with you in the pain. The loss of a family that betrayal dismantled. The loss of a friendship that lasted nearly twenty years and ended in the same season as everything else in 2022. The loss of what you thought was going to happen — the future you had pictured, the relationships you thought were permanent, the version of things you believed you were building toward — and then something completely different happened instead. And you had to grieve the life you thought you were living while still showing up for the life that actually was.

That is a particular kind of grief. The kind without a name. The kind the world does not always recognize as grief because there is no grave to visit. But the loss is just as real. The waves are just as high.

And the waves do come.

On a day in March, Rhondnita sat with grief she could not control. Silent tears. Grandma Georgia on her heart. Her son in law on her heart. The weight of all of it surfacing at once the way grief does — not on a schedule, not with a warning, just suddenly and completely present. She did not try to stop it. She sat inside of it. And out of that sitting — out of that stillness after the wave — came the most honest thing she has written in this entire book.

Grief is like an ocean — it comes in waves and tides — but some days it is just still — I am thankful for the still days.

The wave days are the ones people talk about. The days when the grief rises without warning and takes your breath and reminds you all over again of what you lost. A song. A smell. A Reddit story playing in the background. A birthday that comes around and lands differently now. The waves do not ask if you are ready. They just come.

But the still days.

The still days are what Rhondnita wants to talk about.

A still day is not healed. Let that settle. A still day is not the absence of grief or the end of the ocean. A still day is when you look out across the surface, and it is smooth enough to see across. Things get done. The weight does not surface. You can think about the ones you lost without the wave knocking you down. You can hold their memory and keep moving in the same moment.

But underneath the stillness — you do not know. You cannot know. The ocean does not show you what is beneath the surface on a still day. And so even in the stillness there is a quiet awareness. Not fear. Just knowing. The way someone who has lived near the ocean long enough knows that calm water is still water. That the wave could come at any moment.

And that is exactly why Rhondnita is so grateful for the still days.

Not because they are perfect. Not because the grief is gone. But because on a still day, things get done without the weight deciding how deep the breath goes. On a still day, you can function. You can show up. You can even laugh. And the grief is there — it is always there — but it is quiet enough to let you live alongside it for a little while.

If you are in a wave season right now — this chapter is not telling you to hurry up and get to still. The waves are part of the ocean. You cannot have one without the other. What this chapter is telling you is that the still is coming. It has always come. After every wave Rhondnita has ever survived, the still came. Not permanently. Not forever. But enough. Always enough.

And when the still comes — be thankful for it. Not guilty. Not anxious about when the next wave will arrive. Thankful. Let the still days be still. Let things get done. Let yourself breathe all the way down.

The ocean is not going anywhere. But neither are you.

Grief came in waves. Rhondnita is still standing on the shore.

Still breathing. Still grateful. Still going.

Live It Out

Grief takes more forms than we name. Take a moment to name your losses honestly — not just the ones with funerals, but the ones without. The relationships. The futures. The versions of things you thought were permanent. Name them. Grieve them. Give yourself permission to feel the weight of every kind of loss.

And on the still days — notice them. Be grateful for them. Let them be what they are. A gift in the middle of an ocean that is not going anywhere.

A Prayer for the Waves and the Still

Lord, grief is heavy, and it does not always come with a warning. On the wave days hold me. Remind me that the wave will not last forever. On the still days thank You. Help me receive the stillness as the gift that it is, without waiting for the next wave to arrive. You are in the waves and You are in the still. Help me find You in both. Amen.

Discussion Questions

1. What losses are you carrying that the world has not recognized as grief? The ones without funerals or sympathy cards. Name them here if you are ready.

2. Rhondnita describes the still days as smooth on the surface but uncertain underneath. Have you experienced a still day in your grief? What did it feel like?

3. What triggers your waves? A song, a date, a memory, a smell? What has surprised you most about when grief shows up?

4. Is there a loss in your life — not a death but a loss — that you have not given yourself permission to grieve fully? What would it look like to grieve it honestly?

5. On your next still day — what is one thing you want to do with the gift of that stillness? Write it down as a promise to yourself.

HOWEVER,

The Painful Process of Pruning.

Chapter 11

"Sometimes the strong need to be weak for a moment."

There is something nobody tells the strong ones.

Nobody pulls them aside and says — hey, you know all of that advice you keep giving? All of those oxygen masks you keep handing out? All of that wisdom you speak into other people's hard seasons? At some point, you are going to have to take some of that for yourself. At some point, the mantle is going to get heavy enough that putting it down — even for an hour, even for a moment — is not surrender. It is survival.

Nobody tells the strong ones that. So they just keep going. Keep carrying. Keep showing up. Keep being the one everyone calls when the hard arrives. Keep handing out oxygen masks while quietly suffocating behind the strength that everyone else depends on.

Rhondnita is one of the strong ones. She has been one of the strong ones for as long as she can remember. The one who shows up. The one who holds it together. The one who speaks the wisdom and carries the weight and keeps the class running even when she is barely keeping herself upright. That is not a complaint. That is just the truth of what it means to be the strong one in every room you walk into.

But on a Monday in March — the day before a hard birthday, in the middle of a grief season that was already heavy before that week arrived — Rhondnita said something out loud that she had never quite given herself permission to say before.

I just want to not be strong for once.

Not forever. Not permanently. Not an abdication of everything she had built and survived and become. Just — for once. For a moment. For a breath.

And God took that exhaustion and turned it into wisdom. Because that is what He does with the honest things. He does not waste them.

Here is what weakness looks like on a strong woman. It does not look like falling apart. It does not look like quitting. It does not look like the class stopping, or the work is undone, or the people she loves left without. You know those inflatable figures that wave in front of businesses? Still standing. Still visible. Still there. Just not holding themselves rigid for one single moment. Moving with whatever comes instead of bracing against it with everything they have. That is what weakness looks like on Rhondnita. Still present. Just not carrying the weight of holding everything together for five minutes.

It looks like sitting in the corner coloring while the class still runs.

She is not gone. She is not absent. The class is still going. The work is still happening. But for this moment — this brief, necessary, oxygen-giving moment — she is not the one holding it all together. Someone else has the mantle. And she is in the corner. With her coloring book. And the world did not end.

It looks like a mental vacation. A few days where the hard is still there, but she is not required to solve it. A brief respite. Not irresponsible. Not selfish. Just enough. A moment to stop being the one who carries everything so that she can go back to carrying it with something left in the tank.

Because here is the truth that strong people forget. You cannot pour from an empty vessel. You cannot hand out oxygen masks while you are quietly suffocating. You cannot speak life into someone else's hard season if you have not taken a breath inside your own.

They tell you on the airplane — put your oxygen mask on first before assisting others. Not because you matter more. Because you cannot help anyone if you are not breathing. A barely surviving strong person is not actually strong. They are performing strength. And performance has an expiration date.

Real strength knows when to stop.

Real strength looks at the weight it is carrying and says — I need to put this down for a moment. Not because I cannot carry it. Because I am wise enough to know that carrying it without rest will eventually cost me more than a moment of weakness ever could.

Rhondnita is still learning this. Let that sit for a moment. The woman writing this chapter is still learning it. She does not have this mastered. She is not writing from a comfortable distance of full resolution. She is writing from the middle of it. From a Monday in March. From a grief season that is still active. From a life that is still full and still heavy and still asking things of her that require real and ongoing strength.

And she is telling you anyway. Because the most honest chapters are the ones written from inside the hard. Not after it.

If you are one of the strong ones — this chapter is for you. The one everyone calls. The one who shows up. The one who holds it together so everyone else can fall apart safely. The one who gives the advice and speaks the wisdom and carries the mantle without being asked.

You are allowed to put it down for a moment.

You are allowed to sit in the corner and color while the class still runs.

You are allowed to take the breath you keep handing to everyone else.

You are allowed to not be strong for a moment. Not forever. Not permanently. Just for a moment. Just long enough to remember that you are human. That you are not a machine. That the strength everyone depends on has to come from somewhere — and that somewhere is a person who needs rest and grace and permission to be weak just like everyone else.

Put the oxygen mask on first. Take the breath. The class will still be running when you get back.

And you will be stronger for the stopping.

Live It Out

Where are you handing out oxygen masks without wearing your own? Name it honestly. Then name one way — just one — that you can put the mantle down for a moment this week. A mental vacation. An hour of coloring. A conversation you let someone else carry. One moment of chosen weakness that makes the strength sustainable.

Take the breath you keep telling everyone else to take. Start there.

A Prayer for the Strong

Lord, You know what I carry. You know how long I have been carrying it. You know the weight of being the strong one in every room. Today, I am asking for permission to put it down for a moment. Not forever. Just long enough to breathe. Remind me that You did not design me to carry everything alone. Remind me that real strength knows when to rest. Help me take the oxygen mask I keep handing

*to everyone else and wear it myself for once. I trust
You with everything I am putting down right now.
Amen.*

Discussion Questions

1. Are you one of the strong ones? What does
   that cost you that nobody sees?

2. Rhondnita describes weakness as the
   inflatable figure still standing but not holding
   itself rigid — still present, just not carrying
   the weight for a moment. What does
   weakness look like for you when you allow
   yourself to have it?

3. When did you last take the breath you keep
   handing to everyone else? What stopped you
   from taking it sooner?

4. What is one mantle you are carrying right
   now that you could put down — even for an
   hour — without the world ending? What
   would it feel like to put it down?

5. Who in your life gives you permission to not
   be strong? And if the answer is nobody —
   what would it mean to give that permission to
   yourself?

Part Four: Growing and Giving Well

Congratulations on not giving up on you.

I mean that with everything I have. You picked up this book, and you stayed with it. Through Part One, when hard showed up in your face and told you to quit. Through Part Two, when faith had to carry what your strength could not. Through Part Three, when surviving was not glamorous and was not pretty and was not anything anybody puts on a highlight reel, but you did it anyway. One breath. One day. One however at a time.

And now you are here.

You are not the same person who opened this book at Chapter 1. That person was uncertain. Maybe scared. Maybe already in the middle of something hard and looking for somewhere to land. That person was just learning what hard was and whether they had what it took to face it.

You have faced it. And you are still here.

That is not nothing. That is everything.

Part One gave you the commandment — you are not allowed to stop because it is hard. Part Two showed you who was working on your behalf, even when you could not see the work being done. Part Three taught you how to survive the season you thought was going to take you out. And now Part Four asks you to do something that is only possible because of everything you just walked through.

It asks you to grow. And then it asks you to give.

Not give for the sake of giving. Give well. Give with resilience. Give despite what you are going through because you understand something now that you may not have understood when you first opened these pages.

God doesn't bless a closed hand.

It may not be your season of plenty right now. The hard may still be present. The pruning may still be happening. But giving well means you understand that what God does for one, He can do for another. And keeping your hand closed while you wait for your season does not honor the journey you just survived. It shrinks it.

You did not come this far to close your hand.

Growing and giving well is the fruit of everything that came before it. You cannot give well without the courage it took to begin. You cannot give well without the faith that held you when nothing else would. You cannot give well without having survived the season that tried to convince you that you were done.

The pruning was not punishment. It was preparation. And Part Four is what you were being prepared for.

Different is the beginning of growth not the end of it. Relationship comes before the rule. And the flowers — the love, the words, the presence, the showing up — they are given now. While people are living. While you are living. While there is still time.

Go grow. Go give. Keep your hand open.

HOWEVER,

The Painful Process of Pruning

Chapter 12

"Different is the beginning of growth, not the end of it."

I did not plan to rearrange my classroom. I planned to teach. But somewhere between my first year with fourth graders and everything I knew about how human beings actually function, I made a decision that confused a lot of people and changed everything.

I got rid of the traditional seating.

No more rows. No more assigned hard plastic chairs. No more eight, nine, and ten-year-olds expected to sit perfectly still for eight hours and somehow produce their best thinking. I brought in flexible seating — options, choices, comfort — and I wrote a letter to my parents asking for one thing. Give it a month. If, after thirty days, your child is not comfortable, come talk to me. But give it a month first.

What I did not know was that one father left open house that year, sat in his car, and cried.

Not because he was moved. Because he was scared. Because he looked at my classroom, saw something unfamiliar, and thought — I have made a mistake. I have set my daughter up for failure. Different looked wrong to him. Different felt like a warning. And I understand that. I do not fault him for it. Because that is what different does to most of us before we know better. It shows up looking like a problem when it is actually a pivot point.

A month later, he came back. He found me at back-to-school night, and he said — I doubted you at first. But not now.

And then he did something I did not ask him to do and could not have scripted if I tried. He kept coming back. Every year. At the beginning of the school year, he would walk into that open house and find the face in the room that looked the way his face had looked. The worried parent. The skeptical one. The one whose body language said — What is she doing in here. And he would pull them aside, quietly, and say — I understand what you are feeling because I felt it too. And then he would tell them to trust the different.

He became a witness to something he almost walked away from.

Here is what I told those parents every time different made them uncomfortable. When you work at home, and the task is hard, what do you do? You get comfortable first. You move to the couch. You find the kitchen table. You make yourself a cup of something, and you settle in. You give yourself the grace of comfort before you do the hard thing. So why — why — do we hand children hard plastic chairs and expect them to do their hardest thinking without that same grace?

Different was not the problem. Different was the invitation.

That is what this chapter is about.

Different is not a shortcoming. It is not a red flag. It is not the universe telling you that something has gone wrong. Different is a fork in the road. A pivot point. And at every fork, there is a choice — retreat to what is familiar because familiar feels safe, or lean into what is new because new is where the growth lives.

Most of us have been told at some point — directly or indirectly — that different is wrong. Different made people uncomfortable. Different drew stares in the hallway. Different made a father cry in his car after open house. And so we learned to shrink it. To apologize for it. To sand down the edges of our different until it looked enough like everyone else's normal to stop drawing attention.

But here is what nobody told us. Different is not the end of something. Different is the beginning.

On a Saturday morning not long ago, I did something that felt completely foreign to me. I put the oxygen mask on myself first. For a woman who had spent years — decades — making sure everyone else could breathe before she even thought about her own air, that felt wrong. It felt uncomfortable. It felt like I was doing something I was not supposed to do.

It felt different.

And in that moment, sitting with the discomfort of choosing myself, something came up from somewhere honest and true — different is the beginning of growth, not the end of it.

Because that is what I had been living without knowing I was living it. Every hard thing I had ever walked through felt different before it felt right. The knee healing felt different. The honest conversations in my marriage felt different. Sitting with grief instead of running from it felt different. Writing this book feels different. Every new thing felt different before it felt familiar. Before it felt like mine.

Different is not a warning. Different is a signal. It means something is shifting. Something is opening. Something that was closed is becoming possible.

The father who cried in his car — he gave different a month. And different gave his daughter a year of learning the way human beings are actually built to learn. And it gave him something too. It gave him a testimony. It gave him something to walk back into that room and offer to every parent who looked the way he had looked.

You do not have to understand different to trust it. You just have to give it a month.

Whatever different thing is sitting in front of you right now — the new job, the hard conversation, the changed relationship, the unfamiliar season, the oxygen mask you keep picking up and putting back down — I need you to hear this.

Different is not the end of it. Different is the beginning.

Live It Out

Think about one thing in your life right now that feels different — uncomfortable, unfamiliar, or unlike anything you have done before. Ask yourself honestly — am I retreating from this because it is truly wrong, or because it simply does not feel like what I already know? Give it a month. Give different the grace you would give yourself when the work is hard, and you need to get comfortable before you can think clearly. Sit with it. And pay attention to what begins to grow.

Prayer

Lord, you have never asked me to be comfortable. You have asked me to be faithful. Help me to stop mistaking different for wrong. Help me to recognize that the unfamiliar feeling in my chest is not always a warning — sometimes it is an invitation. Give me the courage to lean into the fork in the road instead of retreating to what I already know. Remind me that you have never once called me to stay exactly as I am. Growth requires different. And I trust you in the different. Amen.

Discussion Questions

1. When in your life have you confused different with wrong? What did that cost you?

2. Think of a time when something that felt uncomfortable or unfamiliar turned out to be exactly what you needed. What helped you stay with it long enough to find out?

3. Who in your life has been a witness to your different — someone who came back to tell you they doubted it at first, but not now? How did that change you?

4. What oxygen mask have you been picking up and putting back down? What would it look like to finally put it on and leave it there?

5. Who in your life is standing at a fork in the road right now — someone who is confusing different with wrong? What would it look like to be the person who comes back, the way the father came back, to tell them to trust the different?

HOWEVER,

The Painful Process of Pruning

Chapter 13

"Rules without Relationship leads to Rebellion."

I have been saying this for as long as I have been teaching. It was born somewhere between studying to become a teacher and actually becoming one, and it has never left me. I carry it like a conviction because that is exactly what it is.

Rules without Relationship leads to Rebellion.

The difference between a rule that works and a rule that doesn't is the relationship built between the rule maker and the rule follower.

That is it. That is the whole thing.

Children don't care how much you know until they know how much you care. And until you understand that — really understand it, not just nod at it — you will keep enforcing rules that nobody follows and wondering why.

I was walking my fourth graders to their resource class one day when I noticed a young man upset outside a classroom. I could have kept walking. Something made me stop.

His teacher gave me a quick version of what happened. He had spilled apple juice on himself and refused to clean it up. She had already called his guardian. From the outside, it looked like a defiant child refusing to follow a reasonable rule.

But I looked at that young man, and I saw something else entirely.

He was a Black young man who had just been ridiculed by his friends because the spill made it look like he had wet himself. His pride was on fire. And nobody had stopped long enough to see that.

I pulled the teacher aside. You are not seeing the context.

There are always two sides. Always. I talked to that young man. I did not tell him his teacher was wrong. She was the adult in that classroom, and her word was law. But I helped him see where his real problem was. It was not the spill. It was not the refusal. It was that Mr. Warren — the custodian — should not have to clean up a mess he made. That was where the disrespect lived.

I gave him a consequence that fit. Two days of recess. Two days helping Mr. Warren clean the cafeteria after lunch. And then I told him — I am not going to remember that I told you this.

I was not going to stand over him waiting for him to fail. I was going to trust him with the accountability and walk away. Because the relationship said he could handle it.

He showed up both days. Without being reminded once.

And then he started coming to my classroom during that teacher's period to do his work. He asked. I had already told her he was welcome — but only if it was his decision. He knew the rules the moment he walked through my door. Come in. Do your work. Do not disturb my class in any way, shape, or form. Because that was not the Mrs. Reed he wanted to see.

He never needed to be told twice.

The relationship made the rules make sense.

The difference between a child who receives correction and a child who rebels against it is not the rule. It is the relationship standing behind it. I never walk up to a child and lead with the violation. I lead with the question. Why do you think I called you over here? Because when the relationship is already built, they will tell me the truth. They will own it. And when the consequence comes — and it will come — I can look them in the eye and ask them who caused this consequence and who should you be mad at. Not me. Not the rule. You made the choice. You own the consequence. And they can receive that from me because they already know I am not saying it to hurt them. I am saying it because I love them enough to tell them the truth.

Think about it this way. You are speeding down the road. You know speeding is wrong, but you do it anyway — until the day you get pulled over. The officer is not mean. He pulls you over calmly, walks up to your window, and asks — Do you know why I pulled you over? No fanfare. No cruelty. Just the simple acknowledgment that you already knew what you were doing wrong. He gives you the ticket and sends you on your way. The consequence was always there. The relationship between knowing the rule and following it is not always honesty. Sometimes it is just the absence of accountability. And when accountability shows up — calmly, consistently, without malice — it changes behavior in a way that fear never could.

Because fear of getting caught is temporary. Understanding why the rule exists is permanent.

I want to tell you about a sixth grader who slammed my door.

My students gasped. I was on the phone with her teacher before she hit the end of the hallway. Send her back. She slammed my door. I am the only one old enough to slam my door, and if I don't do it — you bet not do it.

When she came back, I stopped her at the door. Do you know how to close a door correctly? She said yes. I said, " Show me. I had her open and close that door until I was satisfied. Then I sent her straight back to class and told her to have her teacher call me when she arrived.

The teacher called. The message had been delivered. I never had to worry about anyone slamming my door again.

Not because they were afraid of me. Because they respected me. There is a difference, and it matters more than most people realize. Fear follows rules when you are watching. Respect follows rules when you are not.

Children don't care how much you know until they know how much you care. And they will test every rule you have to find out if that is true.

I have had a sixth grader take her sunglasses off in a building full of lights after ignoring every other teacher who asked — because of the relationship built in the seconds before I asked. I have told a runner that I am not going to stop you from running, just don't disturb my class when you do it — because relationships know when to meet a child where they are. I have stopped a tantrum with a look — because that student knew that coming to Mrs. Reed's class was worse than anything his teacher could do to him.

Relationship built all of that. Not the rule. The relationship.

And I showed up on a Saturday for a student who had already told his mother — Mrs. Reed said she was coming. Not she might come. She is coming. His mother kept managing his expectations because I had said I might. But he was not working with might. He was working with what he knew about me.

I did not know that conversation had happened until after I saw his mother at the event.

But he knew. Because consistency over time becomes certainty in a child's heart. And when a child is certain of you, the rules are not a burden. They are a gift. Because they come from someone who loves them enough to hold the line.

Rules without Relationship leads to Rebellion.

But a relationship with accountability — that is, love with structure. That is the standard held by someone worth following. The relationship comes first. Always.

Live It Out

Think about a rule or standard you are trying to enforce — with a child, a student, a colleague, or someone you love. Ask yourself honestly — have I built enough relationship for this rule to have somewhere to land? If the answer is no, start there. Not with the rule. With the person. The rule will still be there when the relationship is ready to hold it.

Prayer

Lord, help me to lead with love before I lead with law. The people in my care are not looking for a perfect authority. They are looking for a consistent presence. Help me to be that. Help me to stop long enough to see the context before I call something defiance. And when the standard needs to be held, let it be held by hands they already trust. Amen.

Discussion Questions

1. Think of a rule or expectation you have struggled to enforce. Was the relationship in place first? What would it look like to build that before returning to the rule?

2. Has someone ever stopped for you the way you needed to be stopped for — someone who saw your context before they passed their verdict? How did that change you?

3. Where in your life have you led with authority before you led with relationship and lost someone because of it? What would you do differently now?

4. Who in your life needs you to show up on a Saturday — not because you said you would for certain, but because the relationship says you will? What is stopping you?

5. Who in your life needs you to stop in the hallway for them the way Mrs. Reed stopped? What is keeping you walking past?

HOWEVER,

The Painful Process of Pruning.

Chapter 14

"Give people their flowers while they are living — dead people can't smell them."

I have sat in a lot of funerals.

And somewhere between the flowers on the casket and the words spoken over someone who could no longer hear them, a question started forming in me that I have never been able to shake.

Did they know?

Did the person lying there know what they meant to the people standing up to speak? Did they hear these words while they could still feel them? Did anyone stop long enough — in the ordinary middle of an ordinary day — to say the thing that is now being said over a casket?

I decided a long time ago that I was not going to be the person who saved their best words for the funeral.

People may forget what you say, but they will never forget how you made them feel.

That is not just a philosophy. That is a practice. It is something you have to choose every single day in the small, unremarkable moments that do not feel significant until you realize they are everything.

Did anyone tell you you were beautiful today?

I have asked that question to strangers, to students, to parents, to people passing in a hallway who looked like they were carrying something heavy. And I have watched what happens when the answer is no. Something shifts. Something that was closed opens just enough to let a little light in. Not because my words were remarkable. Because in that moment, someone saw them. Really saw them. And sometimes being seen is the flower somebody needed to hold on a little while longer until their breakthrough comes.

Everyone you meet is fighting a battle you cannot see. Everyone. The parent who seems difficult. The student who seems defiant. The stranger in the grocery store who seems short with you. Every single person you encounter today is carrying something you do not know about. And kindness — simple, freely given, no fanfare kindness — can be the thing that changes the weight of what they are carrying.

Kindness should be freely given and not easily forgotten.

I think about the student who struggled with a concept for weeks and finally got it. We did not just acknowledge it. We celebrated it. A full celebration dance right there in the classroom because that moment deserved to be felt, not just noted. That child needed to know that their breakthrough mattered to someone other than themselves. That is a flower. Not roses. Not a card. A dance. Love made visible in real time.

I think about the parent who heard their second grader read for the very first time. The child had been working. The parent had been hoping. And then it happened. Right there. And I got to be in the room when it did. That parent did not need to wait for a report card or a conference or an end-of-year celebration to know their child had done something hard and come out on the other side. They got to hear it. They got to feel it. While it was happening. That is a flower given in the moment it was needed most.

I think about a dear friend's mother who took me in as her own. I tell her what she means to me every time I see her. Every time. Not when I remember. Not when the moment feels right. Every time. Because I know what it costs to wait.

And I think about Grandma Georgia.

I told her I loved her the night before she passed.

I did not know it was the night before. I did not have that information. I just knew that I loved her and she needed to hear it and I was not going to let another day pass without saying it. That is the whole saying right there. Not in a chapter. Not in a philosophy. In one phone call the night before I lost her.

I did not have to stand at her funeral wondering if she knew.

She knew.

That is the gift of giving flowers while people are living. Not for you. For them. So they can carry the weight of being loved into whatever comes next. So they do not have to wonder. So the words are not saved for a room they will never sit in.

You have made it to the last chapter of this book. And I need you to hear something before you close these pages.

You are a warrior.

Not because the hard is over. It is not over. Hard does not retire. It just changes shape. But you picked up this book, and you walked through every however. Every pruning. Every hard season. Every chapter that made you sit still and think about something you had been avoiding. And you made it here.

That makes you a warrior.

This book was never meant to soften the blows or the landing. It was meant to be the parachute. The understanding that makes the jump possible. The reminder that you were built for this, even when this feels like too much. The compass that keeps pointing you back to the one person who can handle all of you — God. Flaws and all. Hard and all. However and all.

You do not finish this book and arrive at easy. You finish this book and arrive at equipped.

So go. Go and give somebody their flowers today. Not tomorrow. Not when the moment feels perfect. Today. In the hallway. In the grocery store. In the classroom. At the kitchen table. Wherever you are when you close these pages — there is someone near you who needs to hear the thing you have been meaning to say.

Say it now.

Dead people can't smell flowers.

But you are still here. And so are they.

Live It Out

Think of three people in your life who need their flowers today. Not someday. Today. It does not have to be grand. It can be a text. A phone call. A knock on a door. A dance in the middle of a kitchen. Choose one of those three people and give them their flowers before the day is over. Then do it again tomorrow. And the day after that. Until it becomes who you are.

Prayer

Lord, keep me from saving my best words for the funeral. Remind me every morning that the people in my life are not guaranteed to be there tomorrow, and neither am I. Give me eyes to see the battles people are fighting that I cannot see. Give me a mouth that speaks life before it speaks correction. And help me to be the kind of person who makes everyone I encounter better for having crossed my path. Let me give flowers faithfully. Let me never wait. Amen.

Discussion Questions

1. Who in your life have you been saving your best words for? What is stopping you from saying them today?

2. Think of a time someone gave you your flowers while you were living — a word, a gesture, a moment of being truly seen. What did that do for you?

3. Is there someone you have lost whose flowers you never gave? What would you say to them now if you could? And is there someone still living who needs to hear those same words?

4. How would your relationships change if you committed to making everyone you encounter better for having crossed your path? What is one small way you can start that today?

5. What would change in your relationships if you committed to making everyone you encounter better for having crossed your path? Who is the first person you are going to start with, and what is their flower?

The Place Where Hard Lands

This space is yours. Every thought, every however, every hard thing that needs somewhere to land — land it here. No rules. No right or wrong way. Just you and the page and whatever needs to be said.

Acknowledgments

There are people who make a book possible and people who make the author possible. Both deserve to be honored here.

To Grandma Georgia and Aunt Shirley — you are already in the dedication because that is where you belong. At the very beginning. Before a single word. You were my safe place, my strong place, and my foundation. Everything in these pages started with what you poured into me. I am living well to honor you both. Forever your Rhondnita.

To my mother, Patricia— I want you to see yourself here. Not in the hard seasons. Not in the complicated places. Here. In the acknowledgments of a book that would not exist without the foundation you built before I even knew it was being built. You raised five kids alone and showed me what doing hard looks like before I even had a word for it. You were my first hard teacher. And everything I know about showing up despite — despite the hard, despite the different, despite the however — I learned from watching you first.

I don't know if you will ever read this. But if you do, I want you to find these words and know that they were always here waiting for you.

You are still my mother. I still love you. And you deserve your flowers despite everything. So here they are. While you can still smell them.

To my husband — you have been there. Through the hard seasons and the honest conversations and the moments that required more than either of us knew we had. Marriage is not easy, and we have never pretended that it is. But you have been there. And that matters more than I can say in a paragraph. Thank you for being there.

To my children — you taught me more about doing hard than you will ever know. You were my reason when I needed one most.

To the village — you know who you are. Every person who poured into me, showed up for me, believed in me, and made space for me to become who God was calling me to be. I carry you with me into every room I walk into. Thank you.

And to every person who picks up this book — you are the reason it was written. I did not know your name when I wrote these pages, but I knew you were coming. I wrote them for you. All of you. Flaws and all.

However, Rhondnita Reed

A Letter to the Reader

You finished.

I want you to sit with that for just a moment before you read another word. You picked up this book, and you stayed with it. Through every however. Every hard chapter. Every moment that made you put it down and pick it back up again. You finished.

That was not an accident. That was a decision. Every single time.

I need you to know something about why this book exists. It was not written from a place of having arrived. It was not written by someone who figured it all out and came back to tell you how. It was written from a place of love and necessity. These are the words I wished someone had told me when I was in my own season of hard. When the pruning felt like punishment and the different felt like wrong and the hard felt like it was never going to end.

Nobody handed me this book. I had to live it first.

This is learned and not taught. There is no classroom for what these pages hold. There is no shortcut through the hard season and no way to borrow someone else's faith when yours feels thin. You have to sit with it. You have to stay in it. You have to choose however when everything in you wants to choose stop.

I know because I chose it. Not perfectly. Not without doubt. Not without days when the best prayer I had was I'm here. But I chose it. However after however after however.

And now so have you.

This book was written from a place of sitting with who I am despite being who I am. Flaws and all. Hard and all. However and all. Not because I am special. Because I am willing. Willing to be honest about the hard. Willing to write it down plain without sugarcoating it. Willing to trust that the next person who needed these words would find them.

You found them.

Which means you were always meant to finish this journey. Not the journey of the book. The journey of your life. The hard that brought you here was not a detour. It was the road. And you are still on it. And that is not a problem. That is the point.

The pruning is not punishment. It is preparation. And you have been prepared for more than you know.

So now I need you to do something.

Close this book. Set it down. And go live what you just read. Not perfectly. Not without hard. Not without however. But with the understanding that you are equipped now in a way you were not when you opened the first page. You are braver. You are more rooted. You are a warrior who just walked through fourteen chapters of truth and came out on the other side still standing.

That is not nothing. That is everything.

Give somebody their flowers today. Lead with the relationship. Put the oxygen mask on yourself first. Sit with the different long enough to find out what is growing on the other side of it. Let your faith be lived and honest and imperfect and real. And when the hard shows up again — and it will show up again — remember what you know now that you did not know before.

Hard is not the end. Hard is the comma.

However,

Now go be you. All of you. Flaws and all.

With love and necessity — Rhondnita Reed